ESCAPE

*A Child's Survival
in the Holocaust*

ISBN 978-1-54399-938-9

Project Editor: Rabbi Beth Lieberman

Graphics and Image Restoration: Richard Glasband Jr.

This is a work of nonfiction. The events and experiences detailed here are all true and have been faithfully rendered as the author remembered them.

ESCAPE

A Child's Survival
in the Holocaust

**PAUL
GRUSZNIEWSKI**

with NEIL LARSEN

I am dedicating this work to you, Mom and Dad, to your son, Yuda, and to all of our relatives in Poland who died so young. It has been my life-long hope to tell our story: a tale of a few poor souls born into a world of unimaginable hate. We did what we could.

In seventy-five years not a single day has gone by that I haven't thought of your struggles and your love. I hope I've remembered them well, here. You are greatly missed and forever loved. *Shalom.*

- C O N T E N T S -

Foreword

Paul Gruszniewski was born in Poland in 1932 and lived through World War II, one of the most violent periods in modern history. He was a Jewish child doing all he could to survive the Holocaust. He is a polite and humble man whose stories are a testament to a young person's incredible perseverance.

These tales, assembled from conversations over several years, may seem remote in time but the look in Paul's eye is of today. The war years, which still shadow his everyday life, shaped a determined and compassionate man. These pages bear witness to Paul's experiences.

Neil Larsen

The Gruszniewskis in Lomza, 1932.
My dad, Isaak, holds Jan and Yuda and my mom,
Meriam, holds me.

- CHAPTER I -

Life in Lomza: The Pre–war Years

1 9 3 2 – 1 9 3 9

On the banks of the Narew River in northeastern Poland lies the town of Lomza. It is set atop a hill overlooking the river amid lush green farmlands that surround and feed the town, then freeze over during a harsh winter. There were about thirty thousand inhabitants there in 1932 when Paul Gruszniewski was born. Lomza's Jewish history dates back to the fifteenth century. In 1932 there were about nine thousand Jews living in the city.

My parents owned and operated a barber shop and a beauty salon located on 8 Dluga Street, and we lived in the back. Our family then consisted of my father, Isaak, my mother, Meriam, and my older brothers, Jan, and Yuda. My parents, as I know, were liberal, progressive Jews, and we lived in a mixed Catholic/Jewish neighborhood. On various holidays they would take us boys to the synagogue located on Senatorska Street next to the Old Market.

My father, Isaak(center) in his barber shop.

My uncle Bernard Cukierbraum owned a pharmacy a few blocks from us and lived with his family in an apartment above the pharmacy. There was a big cellar in the building where he kept a lot of chemicals in various bottles that he would use to fill prescriptions. The pharmacy was located on Kosciuszki Square, a small park with flowers and green grass and benches. I often went there with my mother when she wasn't working in her beauty salon. She would dress me up warm and take me for walks there. I remember her taking pictures.

With my mother at the park.

The Cukierbraums' apartment was quite large and our families ate dinner together there from time to time. They had an upright piano and their son Jacob played it. My brother Yuda played the fiddle and sometimes after dinner the two guys would play music together. Jacob left for France in 1938 to study medicine.

I do remember that some anti–Semitic people with the Lomza city government got after Bernard for something. I don't know the reason, I was a kid. There was another pharmacy in town and that one was owned by a Christian. My uncle was in the papers and he had to get lawyers. I remember my mother and her sister Helen were so worried. The Poles were very anti–Semitic and wanted my uncle out of business, but he fought the charges in court and won the case and was able to keep his pharmacy.

Bernard had a brother, Moshe, whose nickname was Moshak. He was also a pharmacist, and lived in the town of Jedwabne, about twelve miles away. His daughter, Zinka, had moved from Jedwabne to Lomza to go to school.

* * *

Before Passover days my mom would go through a ritual and make all utensils and dishes kosher. She would prepare *matzo brei* for breakfast, and matzo balls and chicken soup for dinner. Bread was not allowed in the house for the duration of Passover.

Sometimes on Fridays she would prepare a large pot of meat, chicken, potatoes, and carrots. I would take it to the baker and he would set it in the oven after the embers burned out and it would stay there overnight. In the morning on Saturday, I would pick up the pot and bring it home. In Yiddish, this is called *tchulent*. My mom, bless her heart, was a great cook.

* * *

The building that we lived in had no running water. We had to go to a faucet a couple of blocks away and carry it back, or buy it from a delivery man, a Jewish fellow who would come by with a horse and buggy and sell it to us by the bucket. One bucket, two buckets.... We had a water vessel in the corner of the kitchen and he would pour the water into it. My mother would bring water into the beauty salon and the ladies would lean back and get their hair washed over a basin, just like now! We did have electricity in the building, which was used mostly by the barber shop and beauty salon.

On the second floor lived the Hepners, a Jewish family who had two children I used to play with, Mika and Goyo. Also living in the same building was Helena Borowska with her family. Her husband, Stanislaw, was a shoemaker. They were Catholics. I became good friends with their son Zygmund, or Ziggy, who was a few years older than me. He played the accordion and you could hear it all over our building! I think some people liked it and maybe some not so much. But he was pretty good! He played tangos, waltzes. His father also played.

Helen Borowska with her two sons, Ziggy and Rysio

Ziggy and I spent a lot of time together. On All Saint's Day we would walk together to the Catholic cemetery where we'd put flowers at his relatives' burial place. On Easter I went with him to the Kapucyn Monastery. The Christian families would prepare a dish called Wielkonoc for Easter and take it to the monastery to be blessed. I also went to the Catholic church with him sometimes and before Christmas I would help him decorate their Christmas tree. He once invited me to join him during Christmas to go to an event at the Kapucyn Monastery. They had a live show (szopka) there and I was fascinated with the decor and the children dressed up as angels. Whoa!

During the winter months we would go ice skating and sledding. I had a good, strong sled, and we used that most of the time. Our favorite place for sledding was called the Kapucynow Hill, next to the monastery.

We could pick up speed there until we reached the Narew River, which was frozen solid at that time of year.

* * *

I started school in 1938, when I was six. It was a public school where most of the students were Jewish. I was happy–go–lucky and did well in class. I did the usual kid stuff––calling each other names and fighting. My classmates called me '*hudzielec*', the skinny one, but I was feisty. I didn't mind it unless I was pushed around. Then I would fight to defend myself, and end up in the principal's office. I remember my classmates Romek Kalwaryjski and Ignacy Klaczkowski and a girl who I was very fond of, Rayka Garbarska.

One winter we were throwing snowballs at each other between classes and I was somewhat inventive. I picked up an icicle and inserted it into a snowball and threw it, not knowing which of the boys it will hit. Well, it happens that my snowball got the principal's son right in the head. He started yelling in pain and all the boys ran into the building. I saw blood gush from his head and got scared. We had been two groups, one against the other and none of the boys knew that I had an icicle in my snowball. It didn't take long, though, for the principal to walk into my classroom after visiting the other classes. When I saw him, I got really scared.

The room was quiet and he asked, "Who is responsible for injuring my son?" At the beginning, I hesitated to raise my hand, but then I thought: *What can he do to me?* I raised my hand and said it was me.

I was sent home immediately with the order to "Come tomorrow with your father." That afternoon I told my parents what happened. They both gave me a lecture and made me promise never to do anything like that again. I was on my best behavior from then on.

On my best behavior!

* * *

When I was six, my father took me to the Polish town of Brest–Litovsk to meet his brother Benjamin and his family. It was really an experience for me, and it was my first time on a train. We arrived there and I was introduced to the family. He had three or four sons that were all older than me, and they took me around and showed me the neighborhood. Their house was small. When it came time to go to bed, they had the boys and me sleep outside. It was an unusual experience but it was very nice weather and I slept under the stars.

I do remember that the oldest son, Jacob, was preparing papers to emigrate to Argentina. His Aunt Rosa lived there. Being the oldest son he would be able to work and maybe later on bring the rest of the family over. This was in the late 1930s when many Polish Jews were trying to relocate their families outside of Poland.

The next day they took me fishing on the Bug River—it was the first time I had ever been fishing and it was so much fun! It was time for us to go home. When we arrived, I told my mother all about the visit and everything we did.

Fishing on the Bug River

* * *

My oldest brother, Jan, was in high school. They had mandatory military training in public schools that was similar to the R.O.T.C. in America, and he wore a uniform to school.

Mandatory high school military training in Poland, 1936. My brother, Jan, is in the front, sixth from the left.

I remember going to Mloteks for pastry with him and Michael Gayst and my cousin, Zinka. Mr. Mlotek was a baker and specialized in pastries. He was very well known in the Jewish community. It was such great pastry! I remember even now. He had some tables and chairs there for people to sit and have a coffee.

Sometimes Jan or my father would take me for bicycle rides. Jan once took me to the house where my mother's parents, my grandparents used to live. Their names were Simon and Basha Bravman and they had passed away years before. Their house was in Lomza on Polowa Street, next to a Catholic seminary, and it had no regular floor. No wood or linoleum, just a dirt floor. Very poor living conditions. I remember that.

Jan left for the U.S.A. in 1937, luckily, just before the war started. He got out of Poland just in time. He sailed to New York on the M.S. Batory in December 1937. My mothers' sister, Sylvia met him in New York.

I remember when my father took him to the port in Gdynia, Poland. When he returned home that day he brought me a toy tank. It was my first toy, ever! It was a wind–up spring loaded tank and when you cranked the handle, sparks came out. I played with it so much that I don't think that tank lived that long.

I never had many toys but I had a tremendous stamp collection at the time, huge––and I've always loved to garden, too. In Lomza I had a garden alongside a wooden fence that was between us and the neighbor's house. I grew green beans (delicious!) and sunflowers, etc.

There was a billiards hall across the square from my uncle's pharmacy and I went there sometimes with Ziggy. He taught me to play but I could barely reach over the table. They would let us in there in the afternoons when nobody was there.

Ziggy would take me here and he would take me there. We went ice skating and sledding, things like that. When we skated on the lake, I stayed where the ice was safe, but he was fearless. He'd try to get me to join him in the middle but I was afraid and would yell for him to come back. When we sledded down the hill next to the monastery, we'd pick up so much speed that we'd end up on the frozen water of the Narew. Sometimes we would ride together on his bicycle to visit his uncle in Gielczyn, a farmer named Jan Burbutkowski. Ziggy took me out there sometimes to get vegetables for his mother's store.

He'd say, "Hey, c'mon. You wanna go for a ride?"

"Yeah, Yeah." I'd jump on the bike with him and off we went!

The walkway that we took, Polowa Street, passed the blacksmith shop and the Catholic cemetery. Using this walkway, we would ride his bike through the little town of Zawady all the way to Gielczyn, about five miles. Once in a while I would need to stop and take a break because my butt was sore from sitting on the bicycle frame. When we got to the farm, his uncle would give us some green stuff, vegetables. He grew lots of vegetables and he would give us as much as we could put on the bicycle. We would take them back to Ziggy's mother, Helen.

Helen owned and operated a dairy/creamery. She served ice cream and it was Ziggy's and my job to turn the old handle of a wooden bucket ice cream maker that had chunks of ice and salt. One day we decided to invent something so we would not have to use our hands. We attached an improvised gear and chain to the ice cream maker and attached that to his bicycle on a stand. We pedaled until one of us got tired, taking turns. Our system was very clever and operated very well. He was a great guy!

Ziggy gave me quite a bit of input on how to manage in life. I am Jewish and he is Catholic and he talked to me about the anti–Semitism of the Poles. I was just a kid and didn't understand too much but he was very open about it. He was a few years older than me. One of the most important parts of my survival is the fact that I associated quite a bit with Ziggy while I was growing up. He was a very smart guy. I was learning how to survive and I also learned how to act like Polish boy. The word for it in Yiddish is *shaygetz,* a Jew who acts like a Polack.

Radios in pre–war Poland were a luxury. Ziggy and I decided to build a little crystal radio, very primitive, so we could listen to the news. We bought the parts, assembled it, and it worked! We had to install an antenna on the roof. Ziggy climbed up to do it. The owner of the building didn't like it but she let us keep it up. The radio was simple, but it worked and we could listen to the news and what was going on. The news came out that Germany was preparing herself for war. We heard that Hitler entered Austria and then Czechoslovakia. So, we waited to hear just when he would take over Poland. We were able to get the latest news.

*Ziggy and me in 1937. This was my garden next to our apartment
and those huge leaves are sunflower plants that I planted. You can
see some of the sunflowers.*

War

On September 1st, 1939, World War II began with Germany's invasion of Poland. Lomza, located in eastern Poland, was in peril from the first day and most of the inhabitants fled the oncoming attack.

Prior to the bombardment, the German aircraft dropped all kinds of booby traps designed to kill people. What looked like boxes of chocolate candies and toys were exploding mines. They were specially designed for the civilian population. For kids. Kids would pick them up because they looked like shiny toys or chocolate candy bars and they would blow up. I was warned not to touch them if I saw them.

Our family escaped the city during the bombardment of Lomza by the German Luftwaffe and were given shelter by Ziggy's uncle, Mr. Burbutkowski, who let us live in a cellar adjacent to his farm house in Gielczyn until the bombardment stopped. The cellar had brick walls and it was very primitive. The attack on Lomza lasted about a week. First we heard the tanks coming and then the explosions. Germany came from the northwest and just marched through Poland.

On September 3rd the Luftwaffe began the first of several aerial assaults on Lomza and the town was set on fire. German artillery joined the attack and over one thousand Lomza citizens were killed. On September 10th, the

Polish Army abandoned their positions and widespread looting broke out
until the German ground forces moved in, unopposed, two days later.

We heard the fighting stop and carefully made our way back into
Lomza. It was a horrible sight. Buildings destroyed, some of them still
smoldering, the stench of burned bodies, and dead horses in the street. A
lot of the buildings at that time were wooden structures and they would
burn like a box of matches. On top of that, most of the shops that were
still standing had been looted. The German military was already there, the
Shutz Police and the Sirhereitz Police Gestapo. Luckily, our apartment and
barber shop were not damaged, although three buildings across the street
from us were destroyed. We also had good security bars and our furniture
and barber shop equipment were intact, as we had left them. My uncle's
pharmacy and home, and in fact his whole block, was destroyed by bombardment and fire. All the chemicals he had stored in the basement to make
prescriptions were burned. The mayor ordered an immediate cleanup of
the city. I tried to help with the difficult job of digging up charred bodies
but I couldn't take the horrible smells and sights.

It was difficult to buy anything because of the fires and looting. The
baker, Mr. Mlotek, started to function. His bakery was destroyed but his
oven somehow survived, and he started baking bread. There were long
lines of people out front. We had a small food supply, but it did not last. I
decided to go to Koszary of 33 Pulk one day, where the German army was
stationed. I went to the Nazi guard in front and asked him for some bread
and to my surprise, he gave me some! With my blue eyes and blond hair, I
guess they didn't suspect me of being Jewish. My parents were surprised to
see me come back with some bread. They were not the loaves as we know
sold by bakeries, but kind of a square wrapped in paper. Whenever I go to
a deli today, I see almost the same dark pumpernickel which takes me back
a few years. Those were the days!

When Stalin and Hitler divided Poland on September 29th, we found ourselves in the Russian occupied zone. The scenario changed. The Jewish
population I might say was treated well but the Russians kept an eye on us.
They were afraid of the Jewish activists from various organizations and the
intelligentsia from the community. They didn't want them interfering with
their politics in occupied Poland. The Russian Politburo/NKVD picked up
many of them one night and put them on a train and sent them deep onto
Russia. I remember that part very well. I had a math teacher in school I
really liked (it was one of my favorite subjects). One day she stopped coming to school. We found out that she and her husband and kids were all sent
to Siberia. I think her husband was a member of a Zionist organization.
The majority of these people died there of harsh labor.

The Gayst family name was very well known in Lomza. The father
was active in the Jewish organizations and his sons, Michael and Walter,
attended high school with my brothers before the war. They were all picked
up that same night and shipped to Russia. Eventually, the sons volunteered
for the Polish Army while in Russia and they both became officers. They
did this so they would be able to get out of Russia and go back to Poland
with their mother, which they did years later. But no one ever heard from
the father again.

It was still hard to buy food. We'd have to wait in line when there
was bread in the store, and there were times when there was no bread at
all. Milk the same thing and meat was practically unavailable. You had to
know somebody in the butcher shop. Our butcher would leave something
for us.

We slowly got into the daily life. My parents got the barber shop
and beauty salon going and things started rolling. School eventually started
up again and I attended with pretty much the same group of kids that I
knew: Romek Kalwaryjski and Ignacy Klaczkowski, Rayka Garbarska, a
boy named Horowicz.

The Cukierbraums, whose pharmacy and home were destroyed during the bombardment, moved to another building in Lomza but my Uncle Bernard never got his business started again.

My brother, Steve, was born during the Russian occupation. It was October 1940, and it was a home birth, in which my mother was assisted by a midwife. I wasn't actually in the room. Yuda was there but they kicked me out because they thought my seeing our mother in labor might have a negative impact on my life! I went to Ziggy's place. Then, they got a hold of me and I returned home. Steve was already looking around at the world. I vividly remember when he was circumcised eight days later, the yells and the crying, and I left the house again!

My mother was very devoted to Steve. He was a small kid for his age and he had a birth mark, a double thumb on his right hand. He was healthy and did begin to grow. When our mother was at work and not available, I would help out, change diapers, things like that.

Unfortunately, I didn't spend much time with my brother Yuda. I was eight and he was eighteen and he had girls on his mind! Because of our age difference, I didn't participate too much in his activities.

The Lomza Ghetto

A u g u s t   1 2 ,   1 9 4 1 –
N o v e m b e r   1 ,   1 9 4 2

On June 22, 1941, Germany turned on Russia, driving its forces out of Poland during the beginning of Operation Barbarosa. Soon, the Nazis occupied all of Poland, including Lomza.

When Germany attacked Russia, it happened so fast, we didn't even hear any fighting from the Russians. The Germans marched in with their military columns and tanks and the Russians just ran away.

During this time, I saw a German flatbed truck parked on the street with a Russian single–engine plane that had been shot down, in the back. People on the street stood around looking at it. The Germans who were guarding it were being very nice and talking to the people. The Germans were making fun of the plane's design. It was made mostly of plywood! I couldn't believe it.

One of the Germans, a pilot, said, "Look how they're building things in Russia these days!" At that time Russian development wasn't very good, they were poor after the Revolution, etc. Russia had not been prepared for the German surprise.

* * *

With the German occupation came immediate danger for all Jews in eastern Poland. In the neighboring towns of Tykocin, Wizna, Kolno, Radzilow and Bialystok, thousands were executed within the first four weeks of the occupation.

In the early morning hours of July 10, 1941, a small group of German Order Police arrived in the town of Jedwabne, only twelve miles from Lomza. They released the prisoners from the local jail. Then, villagers from the town and outlying areas, encouraged and protected by the Nazis, drove every Jew in the town from their homes to the town square, where they were kept and humiliated while their homes were looted. The Germans provided clubs but no firearms to the populace. That afternoon, led by their own mayor, the villagers drove the entire Jewish population, over three hundred men, women, and children who had been their neighbors, into a barn and burned them alive. This shameful series of events is now known as the Jedwabne Pogrom. Although controversy continues to cloud this disturbing episode of Polish history, it eventually became known to the world that the village had murdered almost half of its own population.

The thought of Jedwabne brings me back to a time when human life had no value. The Germans gave the Polacks a free hand. My uncle, Moshak Cukierbraum, lived there and was the pharmacist in town but he somehow escaped the massacre. His daughter, Zinka, had just moved away from Jedwabne to attend school in Lomza, and she also was spared.

A lot of Nazis began moving to Lomza, and some brought their families. They started posting the latest news at a government building on how they were going to deal with Lomza and Poland. In no time, they gave the order to create a Jewish ghetto.

My family was forced to move into the Lomza Ghetto by the order of the German authorities in the summer of 1941. Thousands of other Jews from our city and surrounding communities all had to move, also. We relocated there with a limited amount of belongings and had to leave a lot behind. We hired a guy with a horse drawn buggy. He took the larger pieces like the bed, the mattress, the bedding, and a couch. We couldn't take a chest for clothes and while we were packing I lost my stamp collection and never saw it again.

The ghetto was located about three blocks away from our barber shop and, although I was only nine, I knew the neighborhood well. I knew all of the streets and the side streets before it was the ghetto. On the day we moved, we entered through the main gate on Senatorska Street, by the Synagogue and across the street from the Old Market Square. We were assigned a room by the Judenrat.

The Judenrat was a committee of Jewish citizens established by the Germans to control the ghetto. It included elders and well–known individuals from the community, some rabbis, some not, etc. The Jewish Militia, put together by the Judenrat, acted as police in the ghetto. They had to be young, healthy men and they wore Star of David armbands that were different than the Stars of David that we wore. This was their identification. They were not allowed to carry firearms, but they had sticks.

All the Jews of Lomza, more than nine thousand souls, were forced to move into the ghetto on the same day, August 12, 1941. The inhabitants had to maintain their own community needs within the ghetto and produce goods for Germany while incarcerated there. The entire ghetto was sealed off with barbed wire with only one gate, and no one was allowed to enter or exit without a written permit from the Gestapo.

There were hundreds of Jewish ghettos of varying sizes in Poland, the Warsaw Ghetto being the largest at over 400,000 inhabitants. By the summer of 1941, every Jew in Poland had been murdered, or forced into a ghetto or a concentration camp.

Life in the ghetto is difficult to describe. The five of us were squeezed into a very small room on the ground floor of an old wood framed house. There were four families in the house. The Hepners, who had been our neighbors in the old building before the ghetto, lived on the second floor with their children Mika and Goyo. There were no sanitary facilities, just one outhouse in the back for everyone in the building. At night we used kerosene lamps and candles to see because there was no electricity.

Any water for cooking had to be brought in a bucket from outside. There was a faucet in the back yard. Everyone would go out with a bucket and fill it up and bring it back into their houses. Food was scarce and sometimes we shared things with our neighbors. We had a communal kitchen but everyone was always waiting in line to cook something. It wasn't an electrical stove: it was coal or wood.

Firewood for the stove was very difficult to find. It was not available to buy and you had to get it any way you could. I was supplying most of the wood for us and sometimes Yuda would help. There were old wooden structure homes near us that were uninhabited and practically falling apart. I hate to say it but I used to rip off wood from them, break it away, and run home with it. One time, one of the members of the Jewish Militia caught me doing this.

He yelled at me to stop, then took me to our apartment, where he said to my mother, "Your boy here is breaking off wood from a house." I was so pissed off because the old house was useless. It was a little shed, falling apart and no one could live there.

The firewood that we brought was just for cooking, not for heating. The building we were living in was old and had been lived in a lot. There was no heat or electricity and it was especially tough in the winter. We just used a lot of covers to stay warm.

* * *

The Jewish Militia controls the ghetto. You can see the armbands and sticks. To the right is the remains of the synagogue that I attended growing up. You can also see the barbed wire similar to the barbed wire that I escaped through with my family. It was just down the street that I was shot crawling under this wire, bringing food back into the ghetto.

DER EINTRITT IN DAS GHETTO
IST NICHTJÜDISCHEN PERSONEN
STRENGSTENS UNTERSAGT
DER BÜRGERMEISTER DER STADT LOMSCHA

WEJŚCIE DO GHETTA
NIE - ŻYDOM
SUROWO WZBRONIONE
BURMISTRZ MIASTA ŁOMŻY.

The Cukierbraums were also in the ghetto. They lived a few blocks away from us and we would visit them sometimes but there was no more piano and violin music. My mother's sister, Helen, and her husband, Bernard, and son Chaim were there.

I remember seeing Bernard's brother, Moshak, there, too, the pharmacist from Jedwabne. I never heard him talk about the massacre there but I was just a little kid. He was living in the same room with his brother and all the other Cukierbraums. Six of them. I saw Moshak's daughter, Zinka, a lot in the ghetto, too. She had a boyfriend and I'd see them on the street and at the Cukierbraums' room.

* * *

There was one Gestapo member by the name of Manke (I will never forget his name) and he was the 'godfather' of the ghetto. He was the only one who would come into the ghetto on a motorcycle. I was fascinated with motorcycles. For me this was really something.

On various occasions he would arrive in the ghetto on his BMW and go straight to the Judenrat office. He would order twenty, thirty, fifty people for a work assignment. He requested young, strong people. The German trucks came and picked them up and they would never be seen again. 'Work assignment' was just fictitious. None of them ever came back. These people's families would never hear from them again. The word started going around that they were killing people, healthy people, able–to–work people. I remember it very well. We knew what was happening.

On August 16, four days after the ghetto was established, the entire adult population was ordered to report to the Swinski Rynek (Pig's Market) for a 'selection'. The Nazis read the names of two hundred Jews who were pulled from the formation and taken to the Gielczyn forest and shot. They had been reported as communist sympathizers when Lomza was occupied by Russia.

My brother Yuda was nineteen years old and was supposed to be at the selections, but he never went, and instead, hid in the attic. It was dirty up there, a lot of old broken furniture and discarded items. I covered him up and told him to be quiet and not move around so he wouldn't be noticed if someone came and searched up there. I would lay in the bed in our room with little Steve under me.

There were times when people would be moving around the ghetto then suddenly the Gestapo would show up and go straight to the Judenrat office to order a selection. At that time the word went out in the ghetto to leave your houses. They knew something not good will happen, but not everybody got out.

I will never forget the scenario as I was once standing with some other kids in the ghetto close to the Judenrat office. We looked around the corner of Senatorska Street and saw some Germans riding towards us. Manke was first. He pulled up on his BMW and went straight into the Judenrat office. Then the Jewish Militia came out of the office, marched directly across the street, and started going from house to house, pulling out people from the arms of their families, everyone yelling and screaming. They seemed to be choosing mainly elderly people, some who were barely able to stand. It really stuck in my memory, how those poor people cried and screamed and tried to fight the Jewish Militia. The Jews were assembled on the street in a line, then pushed onto trucks by the militia. They were then covered with tarps so they couldn't be seen and driven away. No one was able to escape. I witnessed this.

I found out that all of them were shot that day at a nearby forest near the village of Gielczyn, and buried in a mass grave. There is now a memorial plaque at that site in the forest. Gielczyn is where Ziggy's uncle, Mr. Burbutkowski, lived, where we used to ride his bike. I didn't tell my parents about seeing this, but they knew about those things that had been going on in the ghetto.

It's horrible to mention, but after these poor people were taken away, some of the kids went out to where the inhabitants were lined up and looked for things that had been left.

One of the kids came back and said, "Oh, look what I found on the sidewalk! A ring! And this, and that."

Those poor people probably knew that they were going to be murdered and tried to leave their gold and other valuable things in the street so that it could be used by someone else other than the Nazis.

* * *

My father was often ordered to go to the German's quarters on the Aryan side to shave and give them haircuts. They were the Schutz Police, or Security Police. When the wives of the German officers started arriving in Poland to settle down, in the better part of town, my mother was ordered to go to the German's wives and do their hair. I do remember that. Yes.

One day my father took me to work with him and he introduced me there and tried to show me off. I was a blond kid with blue eyes and the Nazis were very friendly to me. They seemed to treat my father well, I would say. I don't know everything he went through, but it seemed that they treated him well.

When I walked with my father on the Aryan side, we were not allowed to use the sidewalk, we had to walk in the street. Of course, we each had our Star of David attached to our clothes.

I remember a German lady and her two boys, not quite teenagers, who started yelling at us, *"Alle Juden sind eine gruppe von lausen"*(All Jews are a group of lice). I felt so belittled that I could not do anything about it.

* * *

I don't remember ever doing anything like celebrating a birthday in the ghetto. Maybe other families did but I doubt it. To buy something for an event like a birthday was not in the cards. Mr. Mlotek opened a bakery in the ghetto but he only made bread. He had to build his business up from scratch.

I spent a lot of my time in our room, babysitting Steve while my parents worked. He was one year old and just starting to walk. I was with him most of the time and I was very concerned about him growing up in a Jewish ghetto.

One day I was sitting on the front steps of the house babysitting Steve and catching some fresh air. I heard a motorcycle from around the corner about a block away. Then I heard some gun shots and all of a sudden, from around the corner, I see a Gestapo officer on his BMW motorcycle chasing an individual. He was shooting at him and the guy kept running away from him. The officer was Manke! He was shooting at this guy while he was riding the motorcycle! I immediately picked up Steve and ran into the house. I couldn't believe it!

* * *

With hundreds of Jews arriving daily from the surrounding towns and villages, the Jewish elders appealed to the Nazis to increase the size of the ghetto area to accommodate the growing population. The Nazis demanded half a million marks for this, which was paid, then they denied the request and ordered a selection for September 17, 1941.

On September 17th, all the adult inhabitants of the ghetto had to assemble at Pig's Market, near the old Jewish cemetery, adjacent the ghetto for a selection. My parents told us not to go outside. They left Steve and me in our room, and they went to the square. My brother Yuda hid in the attic. It was quiet outside. Nobody moved through the streets––it was a dead town. I was so scared. All day went by and when my parents finally came back I was relieved and happy, but they were extremely disturbed from what they had just witnessed: the Germans had pulled thirty–five hundred Jewish inhabitants from the selection and taken them into the Gielczyn Forest and murdered them. Period. One third of the ghetto inhabitants. My parents were not talking much. They changed after this, they were different.

–Gielczyn Forest Memorial–
The inscription reads: The site of a bloodbath of about 3,000 Jewish
inhabitants from Lomza County, slain by the Nazi barbarians in
1942–1943, Gielczyn.

* * *

Later, I overheard them talking about something else that happened that day, about a Jewish family we knew. The lady, Mrs. Kalwaryjski, was a teacher of the German language. She spoke perfect German, and she had a son named Romek who was my friend. We attended school together and our families were forced into the ghetto at the same time. I would see them there from time to time. One of the Gestapo officers felt sorry for the mother. He had a weakness for her and she was able to communicate well with him in German. He might have been romantically involved with her. He was one of the Germans who made the selections and he arranged for special treatment for her and her son.

When the Jews were in the selection that day, the officer took her and pulled her out. She and her son were put in a group off to the side that was not taken to the forest. When things quieted down, Romek and his mother left the ghetto. We never saw them again. Mrs. Kalwaryjski had been married and I heard that her husband was later killed. Maybe she was given the choice to save her son. I don't know.

*   *   *

The Judenrat managed to establish an orphanage and a home for the elderly in the ghetto, but schools were forbidden. During the winter of 1941–1942, epidemics of typhus and dysentery broke out due to starvation and almost all those affected died.

Food was in very short supply. Once in a while I would sneak out from the ghetto to smuggle in food. I always did this alone. My favorite crossing was the barbed wire near Peltins House, which was a part of the ghetto. It was a three story building. Adjacent to the building were ruins from houses destroyed during the bombardment. It was a good place to hide before sneaking through. There was a long wall across from the Old Market Square, then the barbed wire started. I snuck out where the wire started.

I snuck out of the ghetto one day in order to bring back food for our family. On my return trip to sneak back in, I found myself in the Old Market Place near Peltins House. I usually would watch out and look for the German guards because they would walk this street with a Polish assistant. This time, I don't know what I was thinking about. I guess I was starved and hungry and my senses weren't with me. I walked towards the wire and heard yelling.

I turned and saw a German guard yelling, "Halt! Halt!" He was yelling at me!

I don't remember what food I was carrying but I dropped everything and ran. When I was close to the wire I heard some shots and I realized that they were shooting at me. People were still walking on that street. I ran and dove under the barbed wire, which was stretched over a sidewalk. I got hung up in the wire and couldn't get through. Then noticed I was bleeding from my right knee. I don't remember feeling it, but I got shot! My other leg got scraped up in the wire and my clothes were torn, but finally I managed to crawl out and get away.

I was scared the guards would come into the ghetto looking for me and I ran back to our apartment. My mother wiped off the blood and wrapped up my knee and we left quickly to my Uncle Bernard's apartment. It was a few blocks away but we went by side streets so the Germans would not spot me again. My uncle fixed me up, cleaned up the wound, and put some powder on it that slows down infection. He didn't have any stitching equipment so the powder was the best he could do. They didn't take me to the hospital because they thought the Germans might look for me there or follow the blood trail to our apartment or to our floor. I limped around after this.

Around that time, I heard my parents talking about the Hepners upstairs. Mr. Hepner had been picked up by the Gestapo one day and hadn't come back. His wife went to the Gestapo to find out about her husband and she also disappeared. Although it was a dangerous thing for her to do, she had no other choice. Maybe she thought she could bribe them. Neither one of them was ever seen again. A brother of Mr. Hepner, Dr. Hepner, took care of their kids, Mika and Goyo.

* * *

There was a hill that I used to go to in the ghetto. There were not too many bushes or trees around and if you looked out from a small cliff, you could see farmlands and the Narew River. It was a very well-known spot. I would sit up there quite often, dreaming to be free. I could see the highway down below which was outside the ghetto and how people were enjoying their freedom. They were walking and riding their horse drawn carriages. Their lives were going on, but there was no hope for us in the ghetto with the Nazis there.

Zinka Cukierbraum at play with my brother Jan in Lomza,
overlooking the Narew River in 1936. Five years later I visited this
spot when it was part of the Lomza Ghetto. I would sit up there
quite often and I could see the highway down below and how people
were enjoying their freedom.

After about a year in the ghetto, we were able to move to a slightly bigger room, in Peltins House, the building near where I would sneak out. It was so overcrowded in our first room. Steve was just a little kid and needed a lot of attention, and it was very difficult to live there. I remember that very well. Somehow, my father had some pull with the Judenrat and we got a better location. It was known in the ghetto that he goes to the Germans to give them haircuts and shaves, and my mother did the German's women's hair. Maybe that was why my father was able to get a better room.

Our new room was on the third floor and had one window that looked out at the backyard where the outhouses were. When you go downstairs, in front of the house was the barbed wire that encompasses the whole ghetto. We entered through the back yard door.

Old Market Square

Also in the ghetto were my friends from school, Ignacy Klaczkowski and Rayka Garbarska. I remember I was very fond of Rayka ... well, it was just kid's stuff! I saw her in the ghetto a few times. We would talk and share our thoughts about how our lives had changed, with no school and everything. She was so depressed.

I used to sneak out of the ghetto and see Ziggy, occasionally. He felt sorry for me and asked a lot of questions about what was going on and how it was for us. We exchanged stories. I had to be so careful going to see him, and I would never stay very long. The neighbors all knew me and they could snitch on Ziggy's family, the Borowskis. "He's a Jew, he's a Jew!"

– C H A P T E R   I V –

Escape

O c t o b e r   3 1 ,   1 9 4 2

Word spread in the ghetto that many Gestapo members and SS men had suddenly started to arrive in Lomza. The ghetto population became panic-stricken, because that likely meant the ghetto was going to be liquidated and everyone would be taken to the death camps.

The night of October 31, 1942 affected me enormously and continues to affect me. We heard Germans had ordered local farmers to report early the next morning to a given location nearby with their horse-driven wagons. I saw the inhabitants of our ghetto out on the streets, praying. My family gathered in our room late that evening.

My mother, bless her soul, lit a pair of candles and began to talk to God. She said, *"Sh'ma Yisrael"* (Listen, Israel). *"Gottinu, vo bistu?"* (God, where are you?)

We discussed what we needed to do in order to escape the ghetto, including where to go and who we could rely on to help us.

I ran to the Cukierbraums to check what they had decided to do. When I got there, they were all there and appeared in a state of confusion. They were all going to stay in the apartment except for Zinka and her boyfriend, who were about to try and escape the ghetto. Zinka gave me a quick look. I can't remember if she said something to me but she hugged her parents and left with her boyfriend. I decided to go back to my parents.

I said 'goodnight' to all and left. My two aunts and uncles and my cousin, Chaim, stayed in the apartment. When I got back to my family, Mom was still praying, this time while holding Steve on her lap.

My parents decided not to leave the ghetto. They asked my older brother, Yuda, to take me out of the ghetto and go into hiding.

I asked Yuda, "How can we leave them here not knowing what will happen to them?" I cannot express the feeling that was in my heart. Little Steve was looking up at us. We hugged and kissed them. I was afraid for their safety but Yuda and I knew we shouldn't wait any longer and we soon left.

On our way to the Old Jewish Cemetery where we would cross to the Aryan side, we noticed a lot of people walking the streets, some of them praying in Hebrew and Yiddish, walking like they were in a daze. On our way we stopped and picked up my brother's friend, Edek Goldsztein.

We arrived at the cemetery entrance after midnight. It was quiet there; nobody was around. There was no housing nearby, and the crowds were blocks away. A sheet metal gate covered the entrance from the ghetto to the cemetery, and it was surrounded partly by a brick wall and partly by barbed wire. Some green bushes were next to the gate. We were going to sneak out through the barbed wire.

Suddenly my brother tells me, "Wait in the bushes. Edek and I are going to get Chaim."

I thought that just one of them could go to pick up our cousin, but they both left me. It was dark and I got in the bushes to hide and wait for my brother to come back for me. Well, I waited and waited but they didn't show up. I worried more as it got later. I could not estimate what time it was or how long I was waiting. Did he forget about me? Did he not want me to come with him? They were young adults and I was just a kid. I would probably be extra baggage and just slow them down. It seemed like I waited for hours. I eventually realized that they were not coming back. They had left me there.

I started to panic and couldn't wait any longer. I never saw my brother, Yuda, again. He died at Dachau. I ran as quickly as I could back through the streets of the ghetto to my parents. When I arrived at our room, I caught my breath. They were both in the same sitting position as when I left, the candles burning, and Mom repeating the verses. When I told them what had happened, the only words I heard were "*Oy vey!*" They could not believe that my brother left without me. They were very distraught.

I started insisting that we should leave the Ghetto immediately while we have time, before the Germans surrounded it.

"Once the ghetto is surrounded, there is no chance to get out. It's too late."

Again, they hesitated. I started pleading and begging them to leave. I told my mother that we need to get out and go to Helen Borowska's place.

It took a lot of crying and begging but finally, my father picked up his basic barber tools, then Mom picked up Steve and wrapped herself around him with a heavy shawl. We hurried down the stairs and out the back door, out to the streets of the Lomza Ghetto. I directed them to my spot where I had crossed many times to the Aryan side, on Rzadowa Street, which was near our house, by the Old Market. Before we arrived at the wire I begged Mom to keep Steve quiet. There was a wall next to our building, then the barbed wire started again. We snuck out right there, where the barbed wire started, which was over a sidewalk. This was where I had been shot a few months ago. I spread the wires and held them until my parents managed to get through. My mother crawled out holding little Steve, then my father, then I went through. The next day, November 1st, 1942, the Lomza Ghetto was liquidated.

Now we are on the Aryan side. It was after midnight. There was a curfew and it was very quiet. We came out through the barbed wire on a sidewalk that led to Kapucyn Hill, where I used to go sledding. I could see right down the hill. We snuck away from the ghetto on Rzadowa Street. So far we are lucky--not a living soul around. On the right side of the street is the Kapucyn Monastery, where I had watched the children's Christmas play with the kids dressed up as angels. We walked by it very quietly so no one would see us.

We hurried all the way to Helen Borowska's apartment and never saw anyone. Helen and her family had moved into our place behind the barber shop. I knocked gently at the door. She opened the shades to the window and saw us and, oh boy. She had just woken up and was shocked to see us, but let us in and said that she would help but we could not stay there.

"We can be executed by the Nazis for rendering any help to you."

We knew that. We knew that if a Polack was found to be hiding a Jew, the Germans would take the whole Polish family out and execute them. Ziggy wasn't in the house but her two daughters were there.

My mother told her, "The ghetto is being liquidated tomorrow. We have nowhere to go."

Helen said, "Go to Gielczyn, to my brother Jan's farm. He has that large place and he will be able to help you."

We knew where it was. We hid out there during the bombardment and Ziggy and I visited the place on his bicycle.

But before we left, my parents asked me to go back as close as possible to the ghetto to check what was going on. They could still not believe that the ghetto would be liquidated. It was getting light out and I snuck back near the ghetto, to the corner of Dworna and Gielczynska Streets, about a block away from the entrance to the ghetto. I had a good view. And…oh, no.

A lot of Germans were running around screaming. The Jews were being forced out of the ghetto and loaded into trucks and farmers' horse-drawn wagons. These were the farmers who had been ordered to report to the ghetto that morning.

The Germans wanted to achieve their goals as quickly as possible and the wagons were coming and going. I saw the Jewish Militia running through the streets helping the Germans. A group of Polacks had gathered in front of the fence watching what was taking place. I saw some other Polacks down the street gathering on the Aryan side of the barbed wire. They were making unfriendly gestures and yelling, "Oh, they're taking the Jews away!" They couldn't wait to jump into the ghetto and start looting.

I stayed there and watched for a while but I was afraid to be recognized as a Jew. I raced back and related the scene to my parents––the trucks, the wagons.

We made plans to leave immediately.

* * *

From his hiding place, Paul had witnessed not only the liquidation of the Lomza Ghetto, but the end of the Jewish community in Lomza that had thrived for 400 years. There was a pre-war Jewish population of over nine thousand and then, in a matter of hours, on this day, there were none and they would be gone forever.

We said 'goodbye' to Helen and snuck back out to the street. I remember my mom was carrying little Steve. It was early in the morning, Sunday, the 1st of November, and it was good timing. As we walked, to our luck there was a Catholic church a few blocks away and the Sunday Mass had just finished. It was the Catholic church that I had visited with Ziggy. People started coming out, a lot of people from the surrounding area, city people, and villagers. We sort of blended in with them in the crowd.

It was common to say to each other, *"niech bedzie pochwalony"* (let He be blessed). We left that area with some of them, they were people from the nearby villages who were walking home. We were so afraid, we didn't talk with them, we only said, "Let He be blessed."

Łomża   Sobór

After escaping the Jewish Ghetto, we mingled with Catholics leaving
Mass at this church. "Let He be blessed."

We walked to Polowa Street. My plan was to reach Zambrowski Place, then get to a walkway entrance where a blacksmith's shop was located. This is the route where Ziggy and I would ride together on his bicycle. This time was much different. We managed to get through so far without causing suspicion. There were still other people walking around us who had been in services. As we went along Polowa Street we went by the Catholic Cemetery where Ziggy and I had gone on All Saint's Day to lay flowers on his relatives' burial place.

I was ahead of my parents and my mother was still carrying Steve. We walked past the house where my grandparents used to live, the house with just a dirt floor my brother, Jan, and I had visited.

We were trying to walk separately from the villagers from the church. I was so scared that we'd be recognized as Jews. We got to the village of

Zawady safely but after we passed through, I noticed something in the distance, in the middle of the road. I was not sure what it was, I thought a farmer may have dropped a sack of potatoes or something. As I got closer, I realized that there were three dead bodies lying there. I immediately thought it might be my brother Yuda and his friends. As I took a closer look, I was relieved that my brother's body was not amongst them. My parents did not look. There were still some village people walking near us, but they wouldn't look, either.

We arrived at Mr. Burbutkowski's farm in Gielczyn and we stayed behind his barn for a while. Eventually I noticed him leaving the house and coming towards us.

When he got close, I whispered, "Mr. Burbutkowski, it's me, the Gruszniewski kid. Do you remember when Ziggy and I used to visit you on a bicycle?"

"Oh, yes, I remember you."

I told him, "My parents and my little brother are here. Would you be so kind and let us stay in the barn?"

He nodded without hesitation, then told us to hide quietly between the bundles of straw. We explained that during our escape from the ghetto before it was liquidated, we had stopped by Helen's apartment. She told us that her brother Jan might be able to help us.

He said, "Look, my farm is very close to the road. The Germans often drive by and go straight to the forest. I hear shots and then silence, I'm afraid. You stay here now, between the bundles of hay, and I will come at night and take you to my cellar out in the field, where it's safer."

We hid in the barn until it got dark. At dusk, he brought us some food and we were very thankful and we ate it and talked for a while. Then he took us to the field where he had the cellar, about one kilometer away. Every movement had to be quiet. Not to make any noise. We got to the cellar and then he left us there.

- C H A P T E R V -

A Field Cellar

N o v e m b e r – D e c e m b e r 1 9 4 2

A field cellar is a hole in the ground. Inside the cellar was completely dark. This one had a slope where you climbed down, and the top was covered with branches. Dirt floor, dirt walls and very primitive. The temperature when we were there was usually just above freezing. The Burbutkowskis used it to store carrots, sugar beets and potatoes. We made some room for ourselves in the back. There was a place in one corner that was covered with a bundle of straw. You could slowly push it up to see if anybody was watching you, then sneak out. My mom and I would venture out when it was nightfall and walk to various farmers and beg them to spare us some food. Sometimes we were able to get some food and other times we were chased away, sometimes by dogs.

On one of these trips, I walked in one direction to the village, and my mother walked in another. I went to a farmer's house and knocked on his door. It was dark and night. He opened the door and looked at me and said, "Who are you?"

I told him, "I live in the forest and I am very hungry. Could you spare me some bread?"

And that farmer, believe it or not, gave me a whole loaf of bread. That particular type was round and quite big. When I got back to the cellar, I hadn't realized it but it was frozen solid. It was like a brick! In order to eat it, we kept the bread between our bodies until it thawed out and we could break a piece off. That loaf of bread kept us going for a long time, one little piece at a time.

Some nights our farmer would bring us food--boiled potatoes, some carrots. I also ate some of the vegetables in the cellar, especially the carrots, and the sugar beets, which I really liked. They stayed fresh for a longer time.

The Burbutkowskis risked their lives to hide me and my family. In this photograph taken after the war, Maria and Jan are surrounded by their children, including Alina (left) and Jerry (2nd from left).

Mr. Burbutkowski always warned us to be careful. From his farm-house, he could hear gunfire from the executions in the nearby Gielczyn forest. He said that many of the local farmers had been ordered by the Germans to go to the execution site and dig huge pits in the ground for mass graves. He also gave us more information about the liquidation of the Lomza Ghetto. The Jews had been forced into trucks and horse–drawn wagons and moved in one long convoy from the Lomza Ghetto to a transit camp in the city of Zambrow. From there, they were taken to Auschwitz.

* * *

We stayed in the cellar for about two months, until the end of December. It was a very difficult time for us. We would huddle up together just to stay warm and I would keep my ears open for any movement of vehicles or walking nearby. When the ground is frozen, you can hear the cracking. Some nights it would snow but it would usually melt when the sun came up.

The road that the Germans used was so close that I could hear the engine noise from their vehicles. They were taking Jews to be shot in the forest. I was scared shitless because I was afraid they would be able to track our footprints to the cellar there.

Little Steve cried here and there because he was hungry, but it's amazing that he behaved himself so well. I don't know how he got by. He didn't understand the difficulties we all faced. My mother held him all the time. It was dark and I couldn't tell what she was feeding him, maybe carrots. But my mom was falling apart, emotionally. She would cry and pray constantly, then become quiet and distraught.

One night, when my parents thought I was asleep, they started speaking in Yiddish to one another, saying things not meant for the children's ears. "We can't go on living like this. Perhaps we should commit suicide or turn ourselves in." I got very scared when I heard them say this.

One time when my mother prayed, she began with a challenge. "God, where are You? We are Your people. How can You allow this inhumanity? Why have You turned away from us?"

Little Steve was crying and wouldn't stop, and my father was silent.

I spoke up. "Mom, God is not listening."

My mother just looked at me. Then, she told me that she and my father were giving up. "We cannot live like animals in a hole in the ground. We are starving and cold. There's no way to hide our tracks in the snow leading to the cellar. We can't stay alive in these conditions. We're going to give ourselves up to the German authorities."

She told me that I should leave the cellar by myself, without them. "You are a big boy. If we separate this way, we'll all have a better chance to survive."

I was not prepared for this. I begged them not to give up. I wondered if they were thinking to commit suicide in the cellar with Dad's barber tools and they did not want me to be there. But I did not tell them this. They had decided that I would leave soon, before dawn. I stuck my head outside and saw the snow. It was the end of December.

I hugged them and kissed them. Steve was in my mother's lap. I was so worried for their future and for mine, that I didn't think that this could be our final goodbye. I held on to them as long as I could and then I climbed out of the cellar. I never saw my parents again. They were killed in the gas chambers of Auschwitz soon after that.

– C H A P T E R   V I –

Here I am, by myself.

J a n u a r y   1 9 4 3 – A p r i l   1 9 4 5

Paul was now alone. Crouching in a frozen field at dawn, he had nothing. No food. Not a cent. Dressed in rags and nowhere to go for shelter in the freezing Polish winter. And there was an army of thousands, the S.S., who were hunting down the likes of him. They were close enough that he could hear them. Paul crouched by the entrance of the cellar, out in the open, and started to cry. He was ten years old. He ran a distance from the farm so as to not give away his family's hiding place.

Here I am, by myself. Where to go, now? Avu zol ich gejn? There was early morning light and I decided to go to the nearby forest, a couple of kilometers away. I hid there and thought that at dusk, I should go to Lomza. I was so afraid hiding in the forest. Any branch that you step on gave a cracking sound. It was a scary feeling. I didn't go too far into the forest when I heard a fire. I could smell burning branches. It couldn't believe it. I saw a whole family of Jews gathered around a fire. I didn't remember their names but I knew their faces. They had escaped from the ghetto, too, and they had one son about Yuda's age, and he was nonchalantly yacking and making noise.

I said, "Be quiet! It's the forest. The farmers will hear you and tell the Germans!"

I got scared the way they behaved, like they were back in the ghetto, loud and yacking. The fire was going and they were all warmed up alongside it and I left. I just couldn't stay because I was so afraid that somebody was going to come and pick them up.

That happened on the first day that I left the cellar. It was the only time I ever ran into anyone else who had escaped from the Lomza Ghetto. I was hoping not to run into anyone else. It was scary because they were so noisy. You're afraid of your own shadow out there.

There was snow on the ground and I realized as the sun went down, that I was more comfortable during the darkness of the night. I went into Lomza, back to Helen Borowska's place. I couldn't ask her if I could stay. I knew it was too dangerous. She gave me some of her younger son's clothes to wear as mine were infested with parasites. She also gave me a little cross on a chain and put it around my neck, so I would appear to be a Catholic.

She taught me how to cross myself: from right to left, up and down. I practiced and I was finally able to do it.

I asked her, "Where's Ziggy?"

She says, "He's hiding out somewhere else. He was afraid the Germans might pick him up." They would pick citizens off the street and send them to labor camps. Ziggy was about sixteen or so and bigger and taller than me.

She told me that I would be safer if I left Lomza. She gave me directions to get out of town safely and we said goodbye. Helen was quite a wonderful human being.

I wore this cross to disguise myself.

But I didn't know where to go so I snuck back to the Burbutkowskis' farm and into the barn. I crawled up to the loft above the livestock and hid myself in the hay. Then I started thinking and I started crying. Left alone in the middle of nowhere. At least in the cellar, my family was there. I had them to huddle with. Even when I went out searching for food with my mother, I didn't mind, because I was with her. When I left them, I was cut off from everything. Alone. It is very difficult to describe.

* * *

In the morning I left and carefully wandered that day. At night I passed through the town of Nagorki and saw candles in the window of a farm near the road. I was so hungry that I decided to stop and knock at the door. I was allowed in. When entering, I said, "Let He be blessed." This is a must to say whenever I would enter a farm house. The farmers family was ready for dinner and I thought, "Whoa, I'm right on time!" I told the farmer that I was Catholic and that I lost my parents in the war, etc. During the telling of my story, his daughter came out from another room and my heart almost stopped. She was in my class at school and she knew I was Jewish. Her name was Anna Wszeborowska. Our eyes met but I didn't say a word. She then whispered to her father. He did not waste any time–he immediately turned to me and started yelling and calling me names.

"Get out, you rotten Jew," and on and on.

I jumped for the door and ran out of the house. His dog chased me and I jumped over a fence and kept running until I was sure nobody was after me.

When I finally slowed down to catch my breath, I noticed a stack of hay in the distance. I was very tired from what had happened so I bur-rowed myself in the haystack and stayed overnight. I learned that if you separate the hay about halfway up, then crawl inside, it is so warm!

At daybreak, I took off. Now, I am really hungry. I see another farm-house in the distance. I knock and they let me in.

"Let He be blessed."

They gave me some milk and bread. Finally, I had something in my stomach. He needed an extra farmhand because his son had been taken to Germany for forced labor. I became the helping hand on his farm. I attended to a variety of chores and went church on Sundays with the farmer and his wife. I worked hard but I did not starve.

I was allowed to sleep in the farmhouse, in the kitchen on a bunk with straw. I had a feeling that the farmer was suspicious about me being Catholic regardless of the fact that I joined him in church. I noticed when they went to bed they would leave the door ajar, slightly open. That's when I realized they were watching me. Every night after that, I would get on my knees and pretend I was praying and crossing myself like Helen taught me. They watched me practically every night to see how I behaved myself.

After a few weeks he said, "I'm going to the market. You have to help me take a few sacks of potatoes in to Lomza tomorrow morning."

He said he needed to make some money but I was petrified of going back to Lomza with him. I was afraid he was going to turn me in to the Nazis. I knew that the Poles were sometimes paid a bounty for turning in Jews.

Well, we left the next morning. I was so scared. The closer we got to town the more uneasy I was. I finally asked him to stop so I could take a leak. I remember he stopped the carriage near the Bengelsdorfs Brick Factory and waited for me. I hid in some bushes and watched him to see what he's going to do. He waited for a while but, finally, he sees that I'm not coming back and he started moving towards the city. I was so relieved. It was daytime and I could see people walking on the side of the road. I kind of mingled in with them and got back into Lomza.

But, going back into Lomza, I didn't want to go to our neighbor, Helen Borowska's. I didn't want to expose her to danger after she had been so helpful. I did remember that we had very good friends, Polish–Catholics, the Traczewskis, and she was a dentist. They came to our barber shop and beauty salon and were very nice, distinguished. I knew where they lived and I went there.

She was shocked to see me but let me in. They had a clean apartment and food available and she made me something to eat. I explained to her that we ran away from the ghetto and my parents are hiding out in the village, and I am on my own.

She told me that her husband was in Warsaw, working for the Polish underground. I remember that very well. She instructed me not to repeat this to anybody. Then she told me that she would make arrangements for me to meet her husband in Warsaw.

"My husband will help you, and you will be helpful for them, too."

To travel to Warsaw, you have to take a train. She gave me directions how to do it. I didn't say anything negative, but I knew I couldn't take a train to Warsaw. You have to have a travel certificate and I knew I would be caught without one, so I didn't go. But I thanked her for her offer and for the food. We said goodbye and I went back out into the streets.

While I was by myself in Lomza I was scared shitless that somebody would recognize me! I would avoid walking the street if I saw somebody there that would recognize me, might know me, or maybe knew my family. I had to avoid people. I only went into town a few times.

* * *

After separating from my parents and Steve, I worked on farms in the villages of Turosl, Miastkowo, then to Szczepankowo, Cieciory, and maybe some others. I told the residents my story, that I was a Catholic and had lost my parents in the war. I got used to telling those stories and I got rather good at it. To my benefit, I had blue eyes and looked somewhat Aryan.

When I worked on farms, I took cows to the pasture, plowed the fields, milked the cows, cleaned the stalls, fed the livestock, the pigs.

The farmers would help each other out. Sometimes, families from neighboring farms would come to do some of the chores. Often when we were working, they would sing. They sang folk songs from the villages, melodies, and made up the words as they went along; about perspiring, about how they have to take breaks, things like that. And in between they would say, "Thanks to Jesus."

In the village of Turosl, I attended church with the farmer's family. I think that was in '43…… maybe. I cannot tell you exactly when. I didn't care what month it was. The only thing for me was to stay alive another day, to work on the farm.

I survived for over two years by sleeping in barns and haystacks and stealing and begging for food. I would often sleep in the forest. I'd look for a bushy spot with a lot of needles and, hey, you do the best you can! And I'm listening with one ear if somebody's walking by. It's impossible to walk through the forest without breaking twigs and branches.

Sometimes while I was on my own I had horrible diarrhea that really threw me off. When I would finally find a farmer to work for, I was able to get some milk, fresh milk right from the cow, and I would slowly get better.

To wash my clothes, I'd just find a creek and strip down and wash them! One farmer who I worked for made me some clothes. I watched him cut wool from his sheep, cure it, then spin the yarn and weave it into fabric. He made me a pair of pants and a jacket this way.

I thought of my parents all the time but I didn't have too much hope for their survival. The circumstances for them were so dangerous. My father looked Jewish but mother probably had a better chance to survive because she didn't look that Jewish. She also spoke perfect Polish. You wouldn't differentiate her Polish from any other Polack's. She had taught me to speak Polish well.

There were times when I was ready to give myself up because it was so difficult just to live. I was very depressed and despondent being on my own. I was just a kid. I cried sometimes when I was alone but I knew I had to be strong. With all the work I had to do to survive, I didn't want anyone to think I was weak. I guess the willpower to make it through another day was greater than anything else.

* * *

I was told about a farmer in the town of Cieciory who might need some help on his farm. I went there and talked to him. His name was Josef Malinowski. I told him my story and he took me in. He was married but he had no son of his own and was very patient with me.

It was a small farm and he didn't have too many tools. He showed me how to cut grass with a scythe and even made a small one for me. It's a certain movement with the handle. He would go ahead of me cutting and I would be a few feet off to the side cutting in a row next to him. We would leave the grass out there for about four days in the sun to dry out. Sometimes we'd flip it over so the sun would hit the other side. Then we'd put it in a horse drawn wagon and take it to the barn. I'd get on top of the pile and the farmer would throw me a pitchfork and I'd spread it around. Then I'd cut some of the straw. In Poland they cut straw in small, shredded pieces to give to the livestock. We also put in some chopped up potatoes. The horses and cows loved it!

When I first got to the farm there was a field with tree stumps. Mr. Malinowski wanted to use the field to plant vegetables and he told me to clear it.

It was a big job but he said, "You can do it little by little."

I had to dig out the stumps with a shovel and axe and make sure that I got all the roots.

I plowed the fields, milked the cows, and did other chores. Mr. Malinowski had two horses, one of which was very difficult to handle. This horse tried to kick me in the head with his hind legs once while I was feeding him. It was a good lesson to not walk behind horses. The worst job was removing the horse and cow manure, throwing it out from the stalls, then putting it on a carriage and taking it to the fields to use as fertilizer for the potatoes.

I did things like that, whatever was necessary. It's hard work but you get used to it. I couldn't say no! Even in winter, which was always the most difficult time in northeastern Poland. If the fields were covered with snow,

I'd give the cows and horses hay, a portion in the morning, a portion in the afternoon, then at night, to keep them alive.

Mr. Malinowski was a very religious man and church was an important part of his life. I went to church with him every Sunday if weather permitted it. We would ride in to the next town in a carriage or, if there was snow on the ground, a sled drawn by his horse. I worked for him for over a year, starting in the winter of 1944. During that whole time, I don't remember him ever saying anything to me, wondering if I might be Jewish. I believe he truly thought I was Catholic. But he never asked me. He liked me.

Cieciory was surrounded by forests, left and right. I became friends with the other farmer boys, one who was named Stasio Domanski. We went fishing sometimes. Once we could hear bombardment in the distance. The explosions coming from the direction of the trees got louder and louder. That was when we knew the Germans were withdrawing from Russia. We started hearing engine noise from the forest that sounded like there were columns of tanks there. Motorized equipment that seemed to be only a few kilometers away. When the noise stopped, we made a plan to visit the area. I asked Mr. Malinowski if I could go with the other boys and he told me, "After you finish your chores." My friends left without me and I was mad.

After a while, there was a sudden explosion and smoke. I defiantly told Mr. Malinowski that I was going, and I ran through the forest to find my friends. I arrived at a horrible scene. My friend, Stasio, is on the ground in terrible pain, hit by shrapnel and screaming. Our other friend is torn to pieces, killed instantly by an explosion. There was nobody else around. I ran for help and luckily, I found a farmer with his horse–driven cart. We picked up Stas and took him to the hospital in the cart. One of his legs had to be amputated but he survived. I went to the other boy's house and told his mother what had happened. She was so upset, she was in shock.

As I was leaving I heard her crying, "Why him, why him?" Then I heard her say, "Why not you?"

When I saw Stas in the hospital he told me, "We saw something sticking out of the ground and started pulling it when it exploded. It was a mine."

The Germans had gone along this dirt road and planted mines there when they retreated. This was the engine noise that we had heard.

* * *

The war in Poland was over. I asked myself, "What do I do now? Should I hang around here little longer?" I stayed on a while with Mr. Malinowski because it was safe. And everybody liked me there! One of my friends found an old concertina and brought it to me. I played on that thing and, boy, the songs just came out. We got together and I played it and the boys and girls danced. Regardless of the odds against me, I endured. I survived the Holocaust. To make it short, the Jewish *shkotzak* was very lucky!

– C H A P T E R   V I I –

The Shadows of My Friends

S e p t e m b e r   1 9 4 4

German troops had begun withdrawing from eastern Poland, and on September 13, 1944 Russia captured Lomza, but it was a city in ruins. Five years of war and occupation had left much of Lomza unrecognizable in its destruction, and the reduced population of 12,500 included no Jews.

A few weeks later I decided to go back to Lomza and I hitched a ride with a farmer. When I got there, the Germans were gone and I walked through the streets. The town is burned and in ruins from all the bombardments. I was alone with nowhere to go. I was twelve years old. There are no familiar faces and I see people walking around like nothing had happened....

I looked for the shadows of my friends. Pre–war faces, ghetto faces, but I didn't see any. There were no Jews, period. I felt very uncomfortable. My instincts took over.

I didn't go to see Helen Borowska or Ziggy. They were living in our old apartment and it was filled with memories of my family. It's difficult for me to explain why. I had a mental block against seeing them. Maybe I was somewhat afraid. The trauma I had been through was overwhelming to me; I could never erase the reality of what had happened in Lomza. Helen had done so much for us, and looking at it now, I feel bad that I didn't pay them a visit when I could.

I decided to go instead to the Jewish Community Center in Bialystok to search for my relatives. Bialystok was a large city and there was a large community of Jews there who had survived. Many of them had come from hiding in the forests and countryside. I didn't even spend one night in Lomza. I hitched a ride with a farmer who was riding on the road with his horse–drawn carriage. I would get a lift here, then a lift there, and eventually got to Bialystok, which was about fifty miles away.

At the Jewish Community Center in Bialystok, they greeted me very, very warm. It was the first time that I had seen a Jew in two years! And it was the first time that I had been welcomed anywhere in so long. They immediately made arrangements for me to stay with a family in Bialystok and, as I recall, they gave me some money. I had such mixed feelings. Good things and bad.

As I walked to the family's house I finally felt relieved. I could move around freely, a Jew. I got there and had something to eat and slept in a bed. The family soon moved away and I was assigned another Jewish family to stay with.

They had a son. I slept there, ate there, we used to go the events in the Jewish community for a couple of weeks. I met Shmuel Ismach at the Jewish orphanage there and have remained friends with him ever since. He was also a survivor from a city near Lomza.

I met a woman at one of the events who was from Lomza and knew our family. She had been a prisoner at Auschwitz and she survived. She told me that she had seen my mother and her sister, Helen, walking together in the concentration camp, and they did not survive. In Auschwitz/Birkenau, when people were unloaded from the trains, the Germans immediately separated those who could do work from the others. The others—the littlest ones and the old people—were taken right away to the gas chamber. My mother and Aunt Helen were close to 50 years old. No one I spoke to saw my father. I don't know how long my parents were in Auschwitz before they were pushed into the gas chamber.

* * *

As advancing allied troops closed in on the camp in January 1945, the S.S. used its crematorium in an unsuccessful attempt to burn all documents that would reveal the scope of the horrors they had inflicted. The S.S. staff were the killers in the largest mass murder in human history. Surviving records indicate that between January 13th and January 19th, 1943, Auschwitz/ Birkenau received seven rail transports from the Lomza/Zambrow region. The trains carried over 14,000 Jews from the Lomza Ghetto and surrounding region. Upon their arrival, 1,262 were admitted to the camp as workers and the rest, more than 13,000, were sent directly to the gas chambers. Only 205 of Lomza's Jewish women survived these selections and none of its children. Over one million Jews perished this way, in this place.

There is also to be found in the surviving Auschwitz archives two faded documents with these names:

JANUARY 1943. MERIAM GRUSZNIEWSKI—BORN IN LOMZA, POLAND 1905

JANUARY 1943. IZAAK GRUSZNIEWSKI—BORN IN LOMZA, POLAND 1902

There is no indication of their fate and they were checked off no list. The documents only confirm that, in January 1943, Isaak and Meriam entered Auschwitz.

– CHAPTER VIII –

Yuda

I was not able to find any information about my brother Yuda. Years later, I received some documents from Auschwitz and Dachau *(see Appendix 3)* that helped fill in the story. He had been serving with a Jewish resistance organization and rounded up while in hiding. He was arrested by the Gestapo in Blizyn, Poland on August 5th, 1943. I will never know how he was caught or what happened to his friend, Edek, with whom he left the ghetto. Maybe they were separated or didn't stay together. Yuda was sent to Auschwitz, where he worked as a slave laborer.

Yuda arrived at Auschwitz in August 1943, locked in a cattle car on a train with thousands of other Jews. He was twenty-one years old and unaware that his parents had perished there months earlier. Upon arrival, he was selected as a worker by a camp doctor and thus escaped the gas chamber. He was shaved, deloused, given the clothes of a deceased inmate, and assigned a barracks. He was given a number, 119520, which was tattooed on his left forearm (Auschwitz was the only concentration camp that tattooed numbers on its prisoners' arms).

Yuda was a prisoner at Auschwitz for over a year and then was transferred to Dachau. He left Auschwitz by train on October 25th, 1944, and two days later arrived at Dachau, where he was transferred to a satellite camp, Kaufering. The Germans were building underground airplane factories there because the Allied bombers had destroyed the others. The Nazis were trying to develop their first experimental jet, the ME 262. Yuda worked as a slave laborer, building the Messerschmidt factory.

Yuda was subordinated to Organisation Todt, the S.S. building firm that had constructed the first autobahns and the Siegfried Line, and was notorious for using slave labor, including concentration camp inmates, for their mammoth projects. Albert Speer's twenty-year sentence at the Nuremberg Trials was for heading this organization from 1942–1945, and he was at its helm when Yuda arrived at Kaufering.

The eleven Kaufering camps were satellite camps of Dachau and contained a total of about thirty thousand prisoners. There were no gas chambers and no medical facilities. The sickest prisoners just died. The grass around the camps had been grazed completely by the hungry prisoners. Yuda spent six months here, through the winter of 1944–45, building what the Dachau Archives refer to as 'subterrestrian production complexes.' He was one of thousands of emaciated concentration camp inmates who were marched under armed guard, in their striped prison uniforms, down country roads and through villages every day in southern Germany, on their way to and from the underground work sites. Their daily ration was a bowl of soup and occasionally a slice of bread, measured at no more than five hundred calories in total, which they received at the end of their work day.

In April 1945, before the underground bunkers were finished, the American Army closed in on Kaufering and the S.S. prepared to abandon the camps. The prisoners who were not able to walk were put on two trains destined for Dachau. One of those was unknowingly attacked by American aircraft. Those prisoners who were able to walk, over fifty-two hundred, were sent on a death march to Dachau, about thirty-five miles east. All stragglers were shot.

The U.S. Army 12th Armored Division had no previous knowledge of concentration camps and when the first tanks rolled up to Kaufering the next day, they weren't sure of what they had come upon. A few emaciated survivors, clinging to life, stared out at them. Much of the camp was on fire and they found fifteen thousand bodies, many having been burned alive in barracks. The deaths were due to starvation, typhus, or being burned or shot.

None died from poison gas. They had been worked to death. Historian/phi-losopher Victor Frankl was one of the survivors of Kaufering and American author J. D. Salinger was among its liberators.

It is not known if Yuda was on the death march or a train but he somehow arrived at Dachau on April 27th, 1945. Two days later Dachau was liberated by the U.S. Army, but Yuda was barely alive.

My brothers Jan and Yuda swim in the Narew River in 1936.

Help came too late for him. Yuda's years of forced labor and starva-tion in Auschwitz and Dachau were more than a healthy 23 year–old body could bear. Too weak to be moved after the liberation, he was held at an American medical facility at Dachau for ten weeks, as he battled tubercu-losis and several other starvation–related diseases, probably typhus. On July 11th, he was transferred to the Amberg Sanitorium where his condi-tion deteriorated.

Yuda died on December 18th, 1945 in Amberg, Germany. He was a victim of the concentration camps, something I did not find out until 1986, forty–four years after I lost sight of him in the dark frenzy of the ghetto.

THE INTERNATIONAL RED CROSS REPORTED:

JUDA GRUSZNIEWSKI—BORN JULY 17, 1922.

LIBERATED BY THE AMERICAN ARMY FROM DACHAU CONCENTRATION CAMP (PRISONER #119520) AND TRANS-FERRED TO THE AMBERG SANITORIUM ON JULY 11, 1945

DIED THERE 8:45 HOURS ON DECEMBER 18, 1945.

CAUSE OF DEATH: TUBERCULOSIS OF THE LUNGS, HEART AND CIRCULATORY WEAKNESS.

– C H A P T E R   I X –

Finding Steve

During a visit to the Jewish Community Center in Bialystok right after the war, I met survivors from Lomza whose names were Panicz and Golombeck, and they remembered me.

"Oh, you survived, huh? Your cousin Zinka survived, too. She's in Wrocław."

I was ecstatic that someone else from the family survived. I had seen her quite often with her boyfriend in the ghetto, on the street and in her family's room, then I completely lost communication with her after I saw her the night before the ghetto was liquidated. She escaped, too, and I think her boyfriend made up some fake documents for them that said they were not Jewish.

I took a train and went to Wrocław. At that time, people without a ticket were traveling on top of the train cars and between them. I rode on top and just held on. I was lucky that I didn't fall off somewhere!

Finally, I was reunited with Zinka in Wroclaw. The first thing she told me was, "Your kid brother, Steve, survived. He survived and he's in a Jewish orphanage in Poland."

I couldn't believe it!

She added, "Your parents left Steve with the farmer in Gielczyn and then went into the forest to hide."

Years later, Jan Burbutkowski's son, Jerry, filled in some of the details when he met with Paul:

"After you went out on your own, your parents came to my parents with a little boy, Steve. We lived at the time in this old farm house, all eleven of us. Our farm was located near a busy road and it was very difficult to hide somebody under these circumstances. Your parents decided to find a more secure place to hide far away from the city of Lomza. They left Steve with us. No one in our family could imagine that it would be the last time your parents would see Steve."

Jerry's sister, Alina, added her recollections:

".... from the old memories, from before and during the war––I remember my cousin Ziggy would visit us on a bicycle with a little boy. My recollections are vague, but I'm sure that was you! I remember your older brother, Yuda, better.

When your parents brought Steve to us, it appeared that he was about two years old, about a year older than my brother, Yanusz. I remember how I took care of Steve and liked him very much, like a brother. After your parents dropped off little Steve, they went to the Gielczyn forest, where they worked cutting wood.

I will never forget one scene as long as I live: your mother's last warm hug and kiss goodbye to her son. When she arrived at our farmhouse that day, her face was practically covered with a large shawl–she looked like one of the village farmer's wives. She grabbed Steve in her arms and hugged him and hugged him.

He started screaming, 'Mommy, dear. I love you. Don't leave me.'

That scene got to us all. It is difficult to forget how emotional it was and we all started crying. I think this poor child knew that this was his last goodbye. My Aunt Kasia finally took him away from your mom and carried him to another room so he wouldn't see your mother leave. He remained in there and I could hear him crying for a long time. I will never forget it. We had witnessed a tragedy right in front of us.

It was winter and your parents had mixed in with some of the villagers and were cutting wood in the forest with a German policeman in charge. Somehow those people didn't pay any attention to your mother because she looked like a farmer's wife from the village. She had blond hair and blue eyes. But your father did look Jewish and he looked to be from the city rather than one of the villages. The woodcutters noticed him and started yelling to the German policeman, 'He is a Jew!'

Your mother turned around and told them, 'No, no, this is my husband!'

That was it. They were both arrested. When we found out, my grandmother took a case of barber tools that belonged to your father and hid it outside under a peach tree. On their way by our house, the Germans found it, a leather case with shaving and hair–cutting instruments. They came into our farmhouse and asked us if we have other items belonging to this Jew. We told them no, and said we didn't know him. My mom answered that she saw some people in the garden but didn't pay any attention who it was and they left.

'Those people probably left the barber tools there.'

That saved us. If the Germans would have found barber instruments in the house, that would have been it for us. But your poor parents. That was the end of their hiding out. We never saw them again.

Our friends the Witowskis visited us from time to time, and they fell in love with Steve. They asked if they could take him in, but my parents were afraid to tell them that he was circumcised. When they found out they indicated that it does not bother them.

But before the Witowskis could adopt Steve, people in our village started a rumor that we were hiding a Jewish child. Of course, my parents were very scared because the Germans killed whole families when they found that someone in a family was hiding Jews. Because of that danger, my mom decided to move Steve to relatives of ours who lived in a nearby town, Wysoki Mazowieckie."

The Witowskis took quite an interest in Steve and eventually brought him home from where he was being hidden in Wysoki Mazowieckie. It was just Steve's luck. He was with their family through the most difficult times of the war. The Witowskis managed a horse ranch during that time and the Nazis would go there to use his horses.

Jerry Burbutkowski remembers:

"The farm was near the city. Frank Witowski, who had been a sergeant in the Polish Army before the war, lived there with his wife, Genia, and daughter, Danuscha. We visited them from time to time and saw that Steve was being treated as their own son. He was safe there.

After the Russians liberated Poland in 1945, the entire population of Lomza was moved, and we lost contact with the Witowskis. Later we found out that they had moved to Lodz where a Jewish organization took Steve away from them."

Genia and Frank Witowski risked their lives by adopting Steve during the war years. With their daughter, Danuscha, in the 1930s.

Steve:

"My earliest memories are from when I was about four. The Witowskis had a horse farm. They knew I was Jewish and were taking a huge chance by protecting me. I remember sitting on soldiers' laps (I don't know if they were Germans) and playing with their bullets and guns.

I remember a big battle that took place in the area, towards the end of the war during the German retreat. The Germans were pulling their cannons with draft horses, large horses used for pulling heavy weights. I saw them unhook the artillery in order to use it, tie the horses to trees near our farm, and then we went into a bunker for shelter and a huge battle took place. I remember being in the bunker for days and when things finally subsided we came out and all the horses that had been tied up were dead, probably killed by artillery. Mr. Witowski and the other farmers used their horses to drag away the dead animals to bury them.

Eventually the Witowskis started moving around. In Warsaw, they bought me some new boots. I was so excited about them that I started walking and pretty soon I was lost and couldn't figure out how to get home, but eventually I made it. I was about four years old at the time! The place we lived was a three story building with a courtyard. I remember once looking out from the courtyard and seeing a bunch of people being marched with soldiers around them. This was towards the end of the war. I also remember being near a lake. Mr. Witowski threw me in to teach me how to swim and I've been afraid of water ever since!

After the war, a Jewish organization took me from the Witowskis. I remember being moved to a lot of different places, mostly Jewish orphanages. They sent me to Germany, first to Bergen–Belsen which, during the war, was a concentration camp. After the war it became a displaced persons camp for Jews. There were a lot of young people who had been displaced and many of them were adopted by English families, Europeans, Americans. Pretty soon an orphanage would have very few kids and they would close it. Everyone who was left, me being one of them, would be moved to another orphanage. I remember being in quite a few of them. I got shuttled around for four years, from 1945 to early 1949. Eventually, nobody knew where I was supposed to go. One of the Jewish organizations wanted to patriate me to Israel and I left Germany in 1949 and moved to Israel. After being in several resettlement camps I ended up in a yeshiva, an Orthodox Jewish religious school. I stayed there for a year. I have reserved feelings about orthodoxy in any religion. Whenever you only see your point of view as the only way, everyone else becomes 'the other.'"

Steve at Bergen–Belsen in 1946.

I located Steve in an orphanage in Germany, but when he was moved to Palestine, I lost track of him again and it was back to square one. Thanks to my relatives, Uncle Abraham and cousin Jacob, and my friend Schmuel Ismach, Steve was finally located in an orphanage in Bnei Brak. It was not difficult to differentiate Steve from the other boys. He had a double thumb on his right hand. That birthmark was how they identified him. Abraham and Jacob had gone to different orphanages looking for their lost family member with the double thumb.

I wrote to my brother Jan, who was now living in Los Angeles, and told him that I found our brother Steve. Jan sent a formal request to the orphanage to release Steve to his family, but they declined and wanted to keep him. Then Jan got in touch with his sister–in–law, Rebecca Rosenthal, who was the Nation President of B'nai Brith Women. She contacted the American Embassy in Tel Aviv for help and was successful.

Steve:

> "So here I am in Israel and they find me. The people in America find me, one of the reasons being my double thumb. They start making plans for me to come to America but it wasn't that easy. I first had to go back to Germany for paperwork. I was wearing my yarmulke and in my mind's eye I could see everyone saying, 'What's that guy doing here? I thought we got rid of all of them!' The processing ended up taking a year. I was entered again into more Jewish orphanages and near the end of that year, I developed tuberculosis. I had to go to a tuberculosis sanitorium in Germany to be cured, which I was. And then, finally, I went to America, first to New York for processing for a few months, and then on to Los Angeles, where our brother Jan lived."

Steve had been very lucky to survive the war. But Paul's struggle to reunite with Steve would take years. He was not allowed to leave communist

Poland after the war and he didn't see him until 1960, eighteen years after their sad farewell in a freezing potato cellar.

– C H A P T E R   X –

Searching for the Past

S u m m e r   1 9 4 5

As the Allied victory brought relief to Europe, Polish Jews began the sad task of searching for loved ones, piecing together the lives of a people that would never be the same. It is estimated that at around 60,000 Jews survived the war in occupied Poland, either as inmates of concentration camps or like Paul, in hiding.

Zinka was so helpful to me, I considered her my older sister. When she and I spoke further, she shared more details on our family. She told me about our cousin, Jacob Cukierbraum, who had left Poland in 1938 to study medicine in Montpellier, France, at a college funded by the Jewish organization ORT. During the occupation of France, he joined the underground. In early 1943 he was captured. The French Vichy government turned him over to the Germans, and he was sent first to the transitional camp Drancy, France, and then by train to Majdanek concentration camp, where he died later that same year. I eventually received some documents from the Auschwitz Archives about him.

Cukierbraum, Jacob born on 4–19–1919 in city of Lomza, Poland.

His name is on the transport list departed on day 3–4–1943 with the 50th Transport RSHA Jews from Drancy, France.

Transport counting about 1,000 people was directed to concentration camp Lublin/Majdanek, Poland.

Zinka told me that Jacob's brother, Chaim, and both of my aunts and uncles, all Cukierbaums, were taken to Auschwitz during the liquidation of the Lomza Ghetto and never heard from again. Zinka was the only one of her family to get out.

Zinka with Michael Gayst. Wroclaw, Poland 1946. I was also living in Wroclaw at that time.

* * *

She was a very attractive lady. At the time when I was reunited with her in Wroclaw, Zinka was married to Michael Gayst. The Gayst brothers were from a well-known family in Lomza and were both officers in the Polish Army stationed in Russia. The Russians used the Polish Army to help drive Germany out towards the end of the war and there were many Jews serving with the Polish military in World War Two. The brothers' parents were picked up during the Russian occupation in 1939. The mother and sons returned but their father was never seen again. When the war was over, Michael married Zinka and they moved to Wroclaw, where I would see them quite often.

They eventually got divorced and Zinka started getting closer to the younger brother, Walter. Then they got married! I occasionally visited them, spending a day or two, then going back to school where I stayed in the dormitory. At that time in my life I was concentrating on getting my education.

Zinka told me about other people who were in the ghetto. This person, that person. I learned about the Mlotek Family, the bakers, whose oven survived the first bombing of Lomza and who continued to bake bread. Zinka informed me that in the ghetto, they had built a fake wall in their bakery with a hideout behind it. She said that the family hid in there during the liquidation and survived but were discovered several days later. After the liquidation, someone had moved into the bakery and found Mr. Mlotek and his family hiding in their secret room. They were immediately turned in to the Nazis and never heard from again.

Rayka, the girl I was fond of in school, was taken to Auschwitz with her whole family when the ghetto was liquidated. None of them survived.

When I visited my uncle in Brest/Litowsk before the war, his oldest son was preparing papers to emigrate to Argentina, where his aunt lived. I found out that he made it to Argentina but the rest of the family––my uncle, his wife and the other sons––were all forced into the Brest/Litowsk

Ghetto and murdered there. I don't believe that they were incarcerated there. The Germans at the time were executing Jews when they arrived.

I was in Warsaw and met some survivors from Lomza. I asked about my friend, Romek. His mother had been friendly with a Gestapo officer. Apparently, the officer had taken Mrs. Kalwaryjski aside during the selection, and she and Romek were able to leave the ghetto and were sent to Germany. The officer had false paperwork drawn up and they became Germans. My friend, Romek, had to join the Hitler Youth and he became a leader! And he was a Jew! That's how he survived.

After the war he was pardoned by the Jewish government, at that time it was still Palestine, then he lived on a kibbutz in Israel. I wrote Romic a letter, but he never responded. I assume that he did not want to share details of his experience. That was it! I never saw the guy again. It's a strange story. Their survival was very unique. A Nazi feeling sorry for a Jew. I would say that the officer and Mrs. Kalwaryjski were probably romantically involved, maybe not from the beginning, but eventually. The Gestapo man probably changed his name after the war and could have been pardoned. But, listen, some of the Germans, the Gestapo, did have some heart. I felt that.

- CHAPTER XI -

Poland to Israel to America

1 9 4 5 - 1 9 6 0

After the war, I spent a lot of time in the Jewish community of Wrocław. Many of its residents survived the concentration camps or had been in hiding. Some of them had been partisans and had lived in the forests. Many had served in the Russian Army. There were those who tried to get their property back. I understand they had some difficulties.

There was still a lot of anti–Semitism in Poland after the war. The Catholic Church didn't help much. I could tell that at the time. In fact, the church seemed to be condoning, even inciting anti–Semitic acts by the Poles. The Polish underground was still killing Jews.

* * *

I was bounced from orphanage to orphanage. In 1947, when I was 15, I received a letter from my brother Jan, who had moved to Los Angeles, in which he said to get in touch with the Vaad–Hatzalah office in Katowice. They were organizing to send a group of orphans to Paris. It would be easier to get to America from France rather than from Poland. I went to the hotel in Katowice where I was directed. From there, they sent me to the Vaad–Hatzalah orphanage in Bytom, Poland, a strict Orthodox orphanage that was subsidized by international Jewish organizations. There were three buildings; one for men, one for women, and one for children. We waited there to be sent to France. I had a rough time. It was very strict. My day consisted of praying in the morning, studying Judaism all day, and praying at night––without any other scholastic activities. We were never moved to France and I ended up spending over a year there. For some reason, the Polish government closed the orphanage in 1948 and everybody went their own way. Some of the youngest ones stayed there with a supervisor.

I went to Lodz and got connected with a group of people who were organizing to bring Jews out of Poland into Germany.

I asked them, "Could you help me get to Germany? My kid brother is there in an orphanage, etc."

They said, "Yes, sure, but we need some money."

Of course I didn't have any money, so I went back to Wroclaw, to Zinka's.

After a few weeks, a friend of mine from the orphanage, Szmuel Ismach, got in touch with me and said, "Listen, you should come back here right now, to Bytom. They are organizing a group of Jewish kids from the orphanage to emigrate to Germany."

I didn't know it then but it was an illegal operation. I went back to Bytom and I found Szmuel and a lot of the kids I knew. They were all being gathered in a hotel there. They divided us into small groups according to age, and we boarded a train and headed for the border.

The train stopped at a small town. It was night and we had to exit the train. We assembled in our groups and walked towards the border, separating each group by about ten minutes so it wouldn't look like we were all together. Everyone was supposed to be quiet, no noise. I was in a group with a lot of younger kids, about ten, and I was supposed to keep an eye on them to keep them quiet. As we started progressing toward the border line, the officer on patrol started yelling at us.

"Halt. Halt."

Some of our groups had already gotten across, including, my friend Szmuel. The patrolmen ran over and surrounded us and they put us back on the train and took us back to Bytom.

When we got there they separated me from everyone because I was older, and they shoved me into a holding cell. It was where they put drunks and it stunk of pee and vomit. It was horrible. The littlest orphans were put in a cell near me with a lady from the orphanage to supervise them and I could hear their screams and crying echoing in the hallway all night,. In the morning they put me into a separate cell. That night in the middle of the night, they woke me up to 'interrogate me.'

They asked me, "Why do you want to leave Poland? You're a young man. We need you to re–build Poland."

I told them, "I am a survivor and I lost my family in Auschwitz. I want to be reunited with my brother who survived and is in Palestine."

They said, "We need you here to help build a new Polish government." I just kept repeating my story.

I was in that holding cell for three months. They woke me up to interrogate me almost every night. It was not really interrogation. They were communists and they were trying to brainwash me. And I have to say, without reservation, that the interrogating officer was Jewish! I could just tell.

Finally, after three months, they let me out, but every week I had to report to a Polish police station to prove I hadn't left the country. Again, I went to back Zinka's in Wroclaw because I had nowhere else to go.

She told me, "Oh, you shouldn't have come here. You just got out of jail and you may have been followed!" Her husband, Walter, was an officer now with the Polish Border Guard.

They let me stay for a few days and she told Walter about my story and maybe he could get me out of Poland, but nothing happened. So I went back to school. I found a dormitory which was provided by the Polish government and a school that was for both Jews and non–Jews and I finished high school there.

After that, I went to a technical school that was subsidized by the Jewish organization ORT where I studied basic mechanical engineering, drafting, chemistry of metals and design. The second half of every day I spent in a workshop learning the practical application of various metals. From there, I went on to two years at a prep school, which would get you prepared for the university. I was very involved in being a success. The courses were difficult but I absorbed it all easily.

* * *

While I was a student in the early 1950s, I located the Witowskis in Lodz, Poland. They were the family that sheltered my brother Steve during the war, and had since moved to Lodz. I had never met them, so I took a trip there to finally get acquainted.

During this time, I would also travel to Auschwitz every year to commemorate my parents and other members of the family. I usually went with a friend from my hometown. We would take a train to Krakow, and then a carriage to Auschwitz. As I walked around the camp, I remember having thoughts of my relatives and friends and what it must have been like, how they died in those gas chambers. Aunt Helen, Chaim, Uncle Bernard, Moshak, Rayka. Their families. My mother and my father. Kids from school. Almost every Jew in Lomza. How could it have happened? It's still hard for me to understand why.

* * *

Paul, who had been deprived of school between the ages of nine and thirteen, went on to earn a college degree in mechanical engineering while in Poland, and met and married his first wife, Longina, in Lodz. Together, they had a son, Henry.

While in Poland, he never stopped trying to arrange to be with his two brothers in America. In 1957 he and his family emigrated to Israel, where they lived for three years. Their daughter, Mara, was born there. In 1960, they finally made it to America, settling in Los Angeles where both of his brothers were living by then.

Steve:

"What a relief it was when Paul finally made it! He had to jump through hoops to get to America but it was great to see him. There's not a lot of our family left and we needed him."

Paul:

When I was reunited with my brothers in May of 1960, it was one of the happiest moments in my life. I was learning the English language and I got some work but my marriage to Longina was not able to survive the hardships we had been through. We divorced.

Mara:

"My parents did not have an easy time of it. After they divorced, my dad continued to work in aerospace, and my mother created and ran a successful clothing business. To this day, I still don't know much about my mother's early years. She never spoke about them. I knew that in the late 1930s when my mother was around 4 years old, she and her family escaped the Nazis in Poland by fleeing to Tashkent, Russia. It was a relatively safe area and they successfully hid out there for the duration of the war. My mother, her mother, and several relatives made it back to Poland after the War in 1945. My dad, who was a student in Wroclav in the early 1950s, traveled to Lodz then to meet the Witowskis. This was the family who had adopted little Steve during the War. My mom and dad met during this trip. They soon got married and my brother was born. Mom was pregnant with me when they emigrated to Israel in 1957. My grandmother lived with us in Israel and then moved to Montreal to be with her sister. We moved to the States in 1960.

My brother and I grew up mainly in Los Angeles. I was aware of being different from most of the other kids. We were foreigners—we spoke Polish at home, some Yiddish, even some Hebrew. While I loved twinkies and squishing up white bread and bologna as much as the next kid, the food we ate as a family was not the popular cuisine of Southern California.

As I got older, and learned more about my family's history, I came to be aware of the plight of other immigrants who, like my family, relocated to escape a life of violence and hate. I am an immigrant too. Life is sacred."

Paul:

In the early 1970s I started working at a factory where I met my wife, Vicki, and things began to look up for me. In 1980 I landed a good job at Boeing as a mechanical engineer. Vicki and I were married that year and moved to the Seattle area.

Vicki:

"We met at work. He complimented me on my footwear ('Nice boots')! After I got to know him it was hard for me to imagine what his life had been like. I've never been in that kind of danger, in constant survival mode. I had read *Anne Frank: Diary of a Young Girl* when I was a teenager, and learned about the Holocaust in school. But it was a history class. And then I met this man whose life was so much a part of this. It was hard to believe that I knew someone who went through all of this yet he was such a loving, gentle man. I think about that sometimes, that when children go through some hell when they are growing up, they often aren't very good adults. That's not the case with Paul. He's a gentle man, totally different than what the circumstances may have made him into."

Mara:

"Dad met Vicki when I was seventeen. They were happy, they worked hard, and have made a good life together. She is a loving person, and has been a source of unconditional support throughout my life."

With Mara and Vicki in 2019.

Return to Lomza

1 9 9 8

I returned to Lomza. One of my classmates, Yadja, had a class reunion and the word spread that I survived. Jerry Burbutkowski, the son of Jan Burbutkowski, the farmer who hid my family, was at the reunion, and we eventually started corresponding. He had stayed in Lomza while it was communist, got a degree, and became a prosecutor. Coming from his small village, that was a big accomplishment!

I went to visit the Borowskis. The apartment, our old apartment, was occupied by somebody else. Mrs. Borowska's daughter, Alina, had moved to another place in Lomza. The last time that I had seen Alina was the night our family escaped the ghetto. She was at Helen's the night when we stopped there to ask for help. I located her at her new apartment and we had a very warm reunion. I found out from her that her brother Ziggy–– my good friend in the early years––had passed away under very unusual circumstances. He was killed sometime after the war but Alina didn't want to tell me the details.

I also found out that Ziggy and Alina's father, Stanislaw, did not survive the war. He was picked up on the street by the Gestapo in 1944 and never seen again. I don't know why they murdered him. He was Catholic, just a shoemaker, and a nice guy. I was so sad to hear all of this. I am so lucky to survive that period when they were even killing many Polish Catholics.

Historical records indicate that Stanislaw Borowski received the same fate as thousands of Lomza's Jews. He was shot by the Gestapo in the Gielzcyn Forest in 1944.

* * *

1998, in what was once the Lomza Ghetto. I knew the neighborhood well. I knew all of the streets and the side streets before it was the ghetto.

My parents owned and operated a barber shop and a beauty salon at this location, 8 Dluga Street, Lomza, and we lived in the back.

This plaque pays tribute to the victims of the Lomza Ghetto.

–Lomza Ghetto Memorial–

FROM JULY 1941 TO NOVEMBER 1942 IN THESE STREETS:
DWORNA , SENATORSKA, WOZIWODZKA, ZIELONA, ŻYDOWSKA
– NOW ZATYLNA, AND RYBAKI, THE NAZIS SET UP A GHETTO,
WHERE THEY EXTERMINATED 9,000 POLES OF JEWISH ETH-
NICITY. 3,500 OF THEM WERE SHOT IN THE WOODS NEAR
THE VILLAGES OF GIEŁCZYN AND SŁAWIEC. THE GERMAN
OCCUPIERS ESTABLISHED 15 GHETTOS IN THE TOWNS OF THE
ŁOMŻA REGION. THE TRAGIC FATE OF AROUND 40,000 PEOPLE
LIVING IN THEM LED TO THE EXTERMINATION CAMPS. MAY

OUR MEMORIES OF THEM AND OF THOSE WHO HELPED THEM
LAST FOREVER.

*Helen Borowska's daughter, Alina, with her husband, Jery Just, visit
the memorial for the victims of the Lomza Ghetto.*

In 1998 Vicki, Mara, and I went to the former Lomza Ghetto area and paid tribute to all those who perished there. We walked through the old ghetto streets and passed by the Old Market Square where I was shot by the Nazi guard. I found Peltins House, where we lived the last few months we were in Lomza. I didn't take a photo or go in. There were too many memories for me in there. It's hard to explain but it was not a pleasant feeling. That building was a part of our escape. I walked further and found Mlotek's Bakery, although it had been remodeled and was a little hard to recognize.

We also visited Lomza's Old Jewish Cemetery. There used to be a lot of gravestones, I remember, because, before the war, we kids would go there and play around. Now, people put their trash there and there were just a few pieces of gravestones. One of them had a recently-painted swastika on it. After the war, the ghetto was demolished and new houses built. Many Poles used the gravestones from the Old Jewish Cemetery for the steps in their new houses. It was noted in the Jewish press how the Poles disrespected the cemetery. There is a new Jewish cemetery in Lomza that was also desecrated. I knew the location but I didn't go.

We went out to the Burbutkowskis' farm in Gielczyn. Mara and I climbed into the potato cellar where I had said goodbye to my parents.

Mara remembers:

"The cellar was big enough that you could stand up, about 12' by 12'. It was still being used to store apples and potatoes. Dirt walls, dirt floor and very dark and cold. I was stunned to think that they lived here for months.

The farmer's son, Jerry, also took us to the other side of the property and showed us a pit, a small semi-circle in the ground. He explained that when my dad's family was hiding out, they had also hidden a young Jewish woman and her 3 year-old daughter here. You could still see a pit carved out and it would be covered with leaves to hide them. They lived in this pit for about a week.

Jerry's brother excused himself and went in the house and came back with a small old wooden box that he had saved over the years. He spoke no English but as he held it closely, I noticed he was crying. Inside, there were a few little trinkets and a tiny, tiny red ball. Jerry took it out and explained that this belonged to the child. It was the only thing she had to hold and play with."

When Mr. Burbutkowski checked on the mother and daughter one cold night, they had vanished and he never found out what happened to them. The pit was empty except for this child's tiny red ball.

* * *

Vicki:

"We also traveled to Auschwitz. Paul spoke with a woman in the records center there in Polish, and asked if they had any records of his parents. The woman walked over to a card catalog, pulled out a couple of cards and brought them over to us. The cards seemed old, like they had been typed up in 1943. Meriam and Isaak Gruszniewski. From Lomza. Their birthdays. It was very emotional for us both. There was no other information, no occupation, no date of death. It only confirmed that they were at that camp."

* * *

Yuda was a victim of the concentration camps. I visited his grave in Bavaria in 1997 with Mara and Vicki. The stone reads:

HERE LIES YUDA GRUSZNIEWSKI FROM LOMZA, FROM KZ DACHAU

DIED 14 TEVET 5706

ONE OF OUR HOLY ONES WHO DIED AT THE HANDS OF THE NAZIS.

MAY HIS SOUL BE BOUND IN THE BOND OF ETERNAL LIFE.

BORN: JULY 13, 1922 IN LOMZA

DIED: DECEMBER 18, 1945 IN AMBERG

Mara:

"We took a trip to Munich to find Yuda's grave. We located a young couple who had the key to the small cemetery run by the German government. There, we found my uncle Yuda's marble headstone with the name 'Yuda Gruszniewski' and we laid stones at his grave. That was the first time my dad had been with Yuda since Yuda had told him in the ghetto, 'Wait right here!' and disappeared.

My dad had said to me, 'I was young, but on that night, it seemed to me like I waited for hours for my brother to come back for me.'

But Yuda never came back and it haunted my dad. He wondered, 'Did he forget about me? Did he not want me to come with him? They were young adults, I was just a kid and I would probably be extra baggage and just slow them down. I wish I could ask him, 'What happened?'

My dad wasn't comfortable talking about these things while I was growing up. I never wanted to upset him but I've always wanted to know and he revealed his story, the story in this memoir, bit by bit over the years. I got to know many of the details and began to feel haunted by these events myself. My uncle, my grandfather and my grandmother, for whom I was named, all died in concentration camps. I think of them and hope they are proud of me."

With Mara in Israel, 1959.

"I am certainly proud of my dad and I hope these memoirs will inspire the families of Holocaust victims and survivors to remember their relatives' struggles and, as generations pass, continue to keep their flames lit."

A Family's Tragedy

The tragedy of Paul's family was similar to that of all Polish Jews, 90% of whom perished during the Holocaust. Of his twelve aunts or uncles, all except two were killed in concentration camps or ghettos. He lost most of the people in his life before he was thirteen. Those who survived did so because they managed to leave Poland before the onslaught in 1939.

I was separated from my immediate family in 1942 and did not see those who survived until 1960. My parents and one brother died in concentration camps and the other two brothers survived and went to America.

My mother's sister Helen married Bernard Cukierbraum and had two children. They were neighbors and my closest relatives as I grew up. They all died in concentration camps. Her other sister, Sylvia, emigrated to America before the war.

Bernard's brother Moshak died in Auschwitz with his wife. Their daughter, Zinka, survived and emigrated to Australia.

My mother had two brothers, Mendel and Maurice Bravman, who both lived in Warsaw with their families. They all perished in the Warsaw Ghetto.

Benjamin and Abraham were my father's brothers. Benjamin lived with his family in Brest-Litovsk, where I visited them before the war. Benjamin, his wife and two sons died in the Brześć Ghetto. Their eldest son, Jacob, emigrated to Argentina and Uncle Abraham emigrated to Canada, both before the war.

Postscript

When Paul's parents decided that he should go out on his own, it was because he had shown them such great determination and resourcefulness on their sorrowful journey, and he had a chance of surviving the mounting horrors that they themselves could no longer endure. He did survive, and tells the story of their struggle in a gentle tone, defying the world from whence they came.

Paul has received a distinguished decoration for his youthful bravery. It is displayed on his right knee today in the form of a scar, bestowed on him by a Nazi gunman. It has faded a bit but his memory of these events is sharp and real today, as is the endlessly hopeful spirit that carried him through his terrible journey. As with other Holocaust survivors, the physical and emotional effects of the war can be overwhelming throughout one's life.

* * *

Vicki:

"His memories from the past don't go away. It hasn't seemed to have gotten better or worse over time, he just deals with it every day. There are times when he's more haunted than others, and then he pulls himself out of it. I'll remind him it's over. It's different, now."

* * *

I do suffer in the aftermath, even as I get older. It's difficult to erase it all from my memory. They took innocent people, tore apart whole villages, they wiped out an entire population. And I ask myself,' Why did I survive?' And why did my parents not survive?

I don't walk through the forest much today, but those noises, the crackling and breaking of branches are so deep rooted in me. When I try to write down some of the things that happened, I find myself living the memories again and it becomes terribly difficult to continue. It brings me back to the years of horror when human life had no value. I was just a youngster....

About the Co-author

Neil Larsen is a musician from Los Angeles who is known for his work with Leonard Cohen and George Harrison, among others. He is the husband of Paul's daughter, Mara.

Acknowledgments

I would like to pay a special tribute to Stanislaw and Helen Borowski in Lomza, Jan and Maria Burbutkowski in Gielczyn, and Frank and Eugenia Witowski in Lodz. Their names belong with the other Polish Catholic heroes who saved the lives of those such as myself, doing so at great risk to themselves. They were our friends when it was very dangerous to be one.

A Family Photo Album

My mother, Meriam and her sister, Helen, as children in Lomza.

———————————————

My mom, bless her heart, was a great cook.

Newlyweds Meriam and Isaac Gruszniewski

Isaac and Meriam
My father served in the Polish Army in the 1920s.

Three sisters.
Helen Cukierbraum, Sylvia Portnoy, Meriam Gruszniewski.

My parents enjoy the park in Lomza.

I'm holding my ice skates that would attach to my shoes.

A summer day in Lomza, 1936.
Me, Yuda, and Jan with our mother, Meriam, and her
mother, Basha

Me with my older brothers, Yuda and Jan in Lomza, circa 1935.

A proud Helen Cukierbraum and her sons Yacov and Chaim.

Michael Gayst and Jan with a friend in Lomza.
The sign in the upper left corner is our barber shop.
'BARBER – Men and Women'

Jan leaves for America, December 1937. Me in front, with Jan, Meriam, Isaak, and Yuda.

My Aunt Helen, cousin Jacob, and my mother, Meriam. Jacob left Lomza in 1938 to study medicine in France. He joined the Jewish underground there and was arrested in 1943. He died at Majdanek Concentration Camp. Helen and Meriam were last seen walking together at Auschwitz.

The Great Synagogue in Lomza. It was destroyed by fire in 1939.

Steve during the war.

Steve (center) departs Israel for America, via Germany, in 1949.
With cousin Koby and Gad Frumkin, the chief justice in Israel who
helped bring Steve to America.

These are my father's siblings—Abraham, Aunt Rosa, and Max.

Me and my brother Steve in 2012.

Still farming! With my daughter, Mara.

Appendices

Appendix 1: Maps

Auschwitz: Where so many of my family members and friends from Lomza lost their lives.

Brest–Litovsk: I visited my uncle Benjamin here before the war. He and most of his family died in the Brześć Ghetto in 1942.

Bytom [BE–tom]:I tried to escape Poland here in 1948, but was captured and put in jail.

Blizyn: My brother, Yuda, was arrested here in 1943 and sent to Auschwitz, then to Dachau.

Gdynia: My brother, Jan, departed from here to travel to New York in 1937.

Majdanek Concentration Camp [My–DON–ek]:My cousin, Jacob Cukierbraum died here in 1943 after being captured while working for the Jewish Resistance in France.

Warsaw: My uncles, Mendel and Maurice Bravman, lived in Warsaw with their families. They all perished in the Warsaw Ghetto.

Wroclaw [VROT–slav]:I lived and went to school here after the war.

–The Lomza Region –

Bialystok [Be–ALL–ee–stock]: I came here right after the war. There was a large community of Jews here who had survived the war.

Cieciory [Che–CHORE–ee]: I worked on Mr. Malinowski's farm here for more than a year, until the war was over.

Gielczyn [GEEL–chin]: I hid here in a field cellar with my family for two months in the winter of 1942.

Gielczyn Forest: Thousands of Jews from the Lomza Ghetto were taken here and shot.

Jedwabne [Yed–VOB–nay]: Site of the pogrom of 1941.

Lomza [LOM–sha]: My hometown.

Miastkowo [Me–ast–KO–vo]: I worked on a farm here for a while.

Nagorki: I was chased away from this town by a farmer and his dog when the daughter, a former classmate of mine, recognized me.

Szczepankowo [SHTE–pan–kovo]: I worked on a farm here for about a month.

Turosl [TOO—roshel]: I worked on a farm here.

Zambrow: When the Lomza Ghetto was liquidated, during the winter of 1942–43, Lomza's twelve thousand Jews were sent to a transition camp here for three months. They were then sent by rail, locked in cattle cars, to Auschwitz.

–Lomza, Poland–

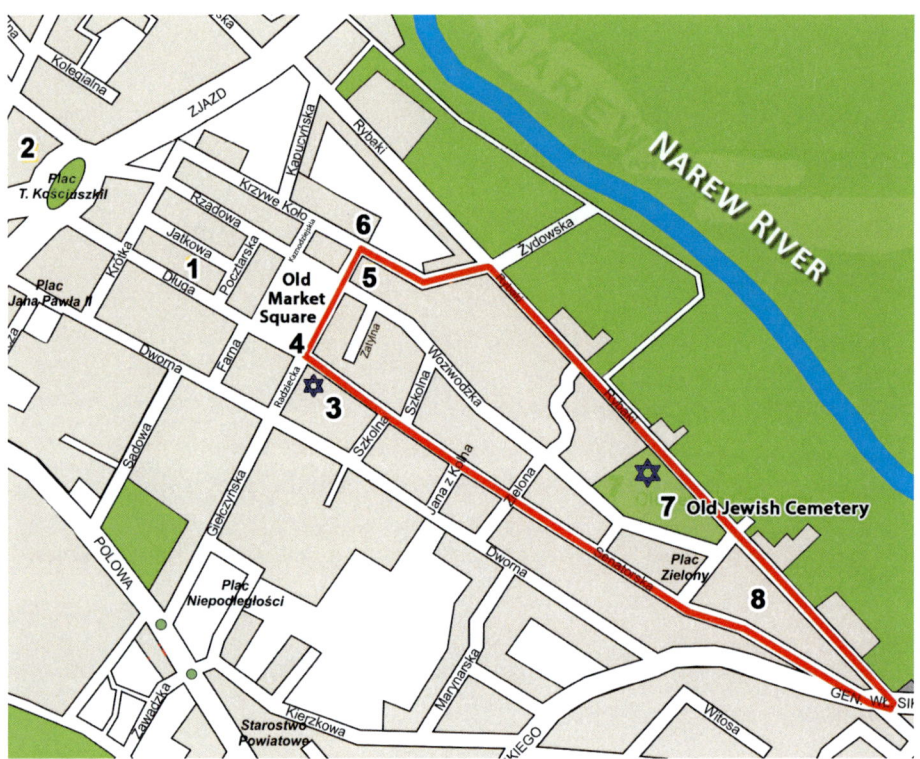

1 – The house where I grew up

2 – Kosciuszki Square: This where my uncle and aunt Bernard and Helen Cukierbraum had their pharmacy and lived with their family.

3 – The Lomza Synagogue: This is where my family and I worshipped. It was destroyed in 1939.

4 – Lomza Ghetto main gate (red border is the ghetto area)

5 – Peltins House: I lived here for part of my time in the ghetto.

6 – This is the barbed wire stretch is where I was shot trying to sneak food back into the ghetto and also where I escaped the ghetto with my family.

7 – Old Jewish Cemetery: The night of our escape, I hid in some bushes here waiting for my brother to come back. I was never to see him again.

8 – Pig's Market: The selections in the Lomza Ghetto took place here.

Appendix 2: People

Borowski, Stanislaw and Helen – My Catholic neighbors before the war.

Borowski, Wanda, Hanna, Rysio, and Zygmund (Ziggy) – The children of Stanislaw and Helen. Ziggy was my best friend growing up until I was put in the ghetto.

The Bravmans – My mother's side of the family. My mom, Meriam, had two brothers, Mendel and Maurice—who lived in Warsaw with their families, and two sisters—Helen, who lived in Lomza and was married to Bernard Cukierbraum, a pharmacist, and Sylvia who lived in New York City and was married to Harry Portnoy.

Burbutkowski, Jan and Maria – This brave couple, a Catholic farmer and his wife in the town of Gielczyn, sheltered me and my family twice. First during the Battle of Lomza and later on, hiding us from the Nazis after our escape.

Alina Burbutkowski – Jan and Maria's daughter. She helped take care of little Steve on her father's farm after our parents were captured.

Jerry Burbutkowski – Jan's son, who I visited in 1998.

Cukierbraum, Chaim and Yacov– My cousins and the sons of Bernard and Helen.

Cukierbraum, Moshak – My uncle, brother of Bernard, was the pharmacist in Jedwabne.

Cukierbraum, Zinka – My cousin from Jednabwe, daughter of Moshak.

Stasio Domanski – Paul's friend in Cieciory.

Rayka Garbarska – She was my classmate until we were put in the ghetto.

The Gayst family and sons Michael and Walter – A prominent Lomza Jewish family. The sons were best friends with my older brothers.

Edek Goldsztein – A friend of my brother Yuda.

Gruszniewski, Isaak and Meriam – My beloved parents.

Gruszniewski, Jan, Yuda and Steve (Simon) – My brothers. Of the four of us, only Jan escaped Poland before the Holocaust.

Gruszniewski, Jacob and Chaya – Isaak's beloved parents

Gruszniewski, Benjamin – My uncle from Brest-Litovsk was my father's brother.

Gruszniewski, Jacob – My cousin from Brest–Litovsk, Benjamin's son.

Mr. & Mrs. Hepner and their children Mika and Goyo – Neighbors of ours before the war and in the ghetto.

Romek Kalwaryjski – A classmate of mine.

Ignacy Klaczkowski – Another classmate.

Mr. Malinowski – I worked on his farm for over a year during the war.

Manke – The German Gestapo officer who controlled the Lomza Ghetto.

Mr. Mlotek – A well known Jewish baker in Lomza before the war, during the Russian occupation and in the ghetto.

The Traczewskis – Our family friends from Lomza.

Witowski, Frank and Genia – A Polish Catholic couple who secretly raised a little Jewish boy, my baby brother, Steve, for over two years during WWII.

Witowska, Danuscha – The daughter of Frank and Genia.

Appendix 3: Documents

MARTYRS MEMORIAL and MUSEUM of the HOLOCAUST
6505 Wilshire Blvd., Los Angeles, California 90048

YAD VASHEM
Martyrs' and Heroes'
Remembrance
Authority
P.O.B. 84 Jerusalem, Israel

דף־עד
עדות־בלאט
A Page of Testimony

ראָס געזוכע צום אנדענק פון אומקם און גבורה — יד־ושם, תשי״ג 1953

שטעלט פעסט אין פארצגראף נומי 2:

די אויסגאבע פון יד־ושם איז אריינצומעלן אין הימלאַבד דעם אנדענק פון אלע יידן, וואס זענען בעשאול. האבן זיך מוטער נשט געוועהן, בעקומסטם און זיך אומסקעגגנסשטעלט דעם נאציישן סונא און זיינע אריייטהעלפער, און די אלעמען, זיי די קהולות, די אַרגאַניזאַציעס און אנסטיטוציעס, וחעלכע זענען חרוב געוואָרן צוליב זייער אנגעהעריקייט צום יידישן פאלק — סטעלן א דענקמאל. (געמעדד־בדד. נומי 332, פון אלול תשי״ג, 28.8.1953)

1. Family name * ● פאמיליע־נאמען **.1**

GRUSZNIEWSKI

2. First Name (maiden name) ● פארנאמען **.2**
(פאמיליע־נאמען פאר דער חתונה)

ISAAC

3. נעבורטש־דאטע Date of birth | Place of birth ● ארט פון געבורט **.4**
(town, country) (שטאָט, לאַנד)

BREST- POLAND | **1902**

5. נאמען פון פאטער Name of father | Name of mother ● נאמען פון מוטער **.6**

NOT AV. | **NOT AV.**

7. נאמען פון מאן אדער פון פרוי און איר מיידלשע־פאמיליע Name of spouse
(if a wife, add maiden name)

8. סטאַבילער וואוינארט Place of residence before the war

ŁOMZA- POLAND

9. וואוינערטער בעת דער מלחמה Places of residence during the war

ŁOMZA- GHETTO

10. ארט, צייט און אומשטענדן פון טויט Circumstances of death (place, date, etc.)

CONC. CAMP OŚWIĘCIM

איך, דער אונטערגעשריבענער I, the undersigned **PAUL GRUSZNIEWSKI**

וואוס וואוינינג (שלער אַדרעס) residing at (full address) **16103 PARTHENIA ST.**
SEPULVEDA, CA. 91 343

קרוב־ישאפט relationship to deceased **FATHER**

hereby declare that this testimony is correct to the best of my knowledge.
דערקלערי דערמיט, אַז די עדות איך האט איך האב דא איבערגענעבן,
מיט אלע פרטים, איז א ריכטיקע לויט מיין בעסטען וויסן.

Place and date **02-07- 80** ארט און דאטע Signature *Paul Gruszniewski*

‎:‫וְנָתַתִּי לָהֶם בְּבֵיתִי וּבְחוֹמֹתַי יָד וָשֵׁם...אֲשֶׁר לֹא יִכָּרֵת‬
" even unto them will I give in mine house and within my
walls a place and a name...that shall not be cut off." Isaiah LVI.5

ביטע אנשרייבן יעדן נאמען פון אומנעקומענעם אויף א באזונדער בלאם.
* Please inscribe the name of each victim of the Holocaust on a separate form.

117

YAD VASHEM
Martyrs' and Heroes'
Remembrance
Authority

DAF·ED דף־עד

A Page of Testimony

P.O.B. 3477
Jerusalem, Israel

39 465

THE MARTYRS' AND HEROES' REMEMBRANCE LAW, 5713—1953 determines in article No. 2 that —

The task of YAD VASHEM is to gather into the homeland material regarding all those members of the Jewish people who laid down their lives, who fought and rebelled against the Nazi enemy and his collaborators, and to perpetuate their memory and that of the communities, organizations, and institutions which were destroyed because they were Jewish.

1. Family Name — GRUSZNIEWSKI
2. First Name — MERIAM
3. Maiden Name — BRAVMAN
4. Date of birth or approximate age — 1905
5. Place of birth (town, country) — ŁOMZA, POLAND
6. Name of mother of the deceased — BASIA/GITTLE LOWMAN
7. Name of father of the deceased — SHIMEN/LEIB BRAVMAN
8. Name of wife or husband — IZAAK
9. Profession — BARBER/BEAUTICIAN
10. Place of residence before the war — ŁOMZA, POLAND
11. Place of residence during the war — ŁOMZA, GHETTO
12. Circumstances of death (place, date, etc.) — 1943-44 AUSCHWITZ, C.C.

I, the undersigned PAUL/PINCHAS GRUSZNIEWSEI residing at (full address) 29029 112 AVE., S.E., AUBURN, WA. 98002 USA
relationship to deceased MOTHER

hereby declare that this testimony is correct to the best of my knowledge.

Signature _____

Place and date of registration AUBURN, WA. 98002, USA. 10-10-92

SECTIONS 1 TO 12 REFER TO THE DECEASED ONLY

PLEASE FILL IN ALL THE INFORMATION IN BLOCK LETTERS.
EACH VICTIM OF THE HOLOCAUST MUST BE INSCRIBED ON A SEPARATE FORM

39.4 7 8

YAD VASHEM DAF·ED דף·עד [יד ושם]

Martyrs' and Heroes'
Remembrance
Authority

A Page of Testimony

P.O.B. 3477
Jerusalem, Israel

1. Family Name GEUSZNIEWSKI

2. First Name JUDA

3. Maiden Name

4. Date of birth or approximate age 07-13-1922

5. Place of birth (town, country) ŁOMZA, POLAND

THE MARTYRS' AND HEROES' REMEMBRANCE LAW, 5713—1953 determines in article No. 2 that —

The task of YAD VASHEM is to gather into the homeland material regarding all those members of the Jewish people who laid down their lives, who fought and rebelled against the Nazi enemy and his collaborators, and to perpetuate their memory and that of the communities, organizations, and institutions which were destroyed because they were Jewish.

6. Name of mother of the deceased MIRIAM

7. Name of father of the deceased IZAAK

8. Name of wife or husband

9. Profession CIVIL ENG'R.

10. Place of residence before the war ŁOMZA

11. Place of residence during the war ŁOMZA, GHETTO

12. Circumstances of death (place, date, etc.) 12-18-1945 C.C. DACHAU

I, the undersigned PAUL GEUSZNIEWSKI
residing at (full address) 29029-112 AVE., S.E., AUBURN, WA. 98002, U.S.A.
relationship to deceased BROTHER

hereby declare that this testimony is correct to the best of my knowledge.

Signature

Place and date of registration AUBURN, WA. 98002, USA. 10-10-92

וְנָתַתִּי לָהֶם בְּבֵיתִי וּבְחוֹמֹתַי יָד וָשֵׁם... אֲשֶׁר לֹא יִכָּרֵת
...even unto them will I give in mine house and within my walls a place and a name, ... that shall not be cut off.

PLEASE FILL IN ALL THE INFORMATION IN BLOCK LETTERS.
EACH VICTIM OF THE HOLOCAUST MUST BE INSCRIBED ON A SEPARATE FORM

I watched Yuda disappear into the night on the eve of the Lomza Ghetto liquidation in 1942, and never found out what happened to him until I received these letters in 1986:

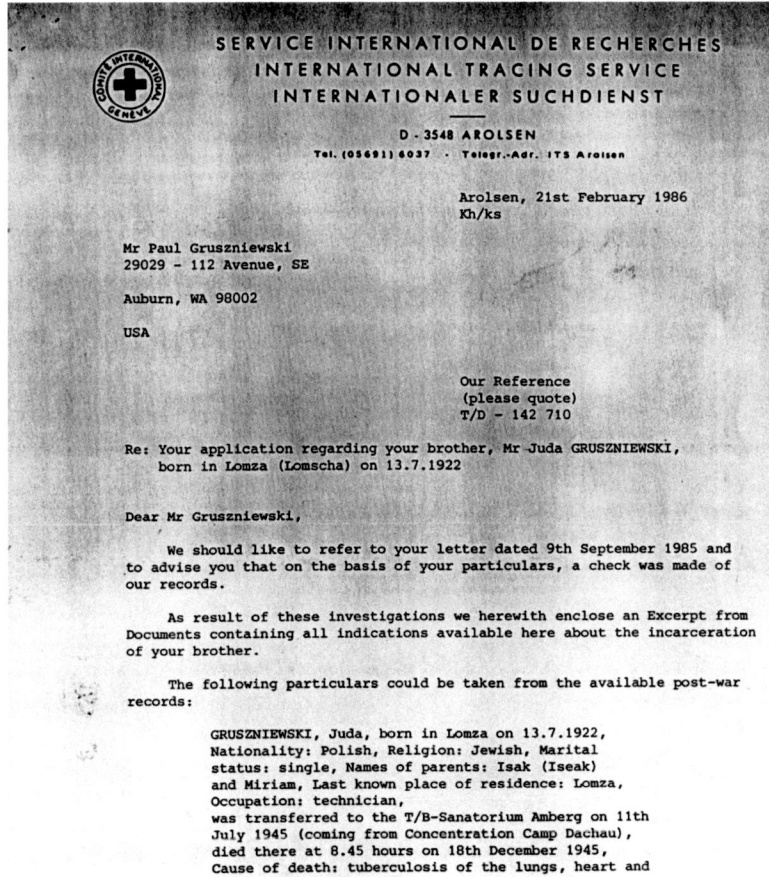

SERVICE INTERNATIONAL DE RECHERCHES
INTERNATIONAL TRACING SERVICE
INTERNATIONALER SUCHDIENST

D - 3548 AROLSEN
Tel. (05691) 6037 · Telegr.-Adr. ITS Arolsen

Arolsen, 21st February 1986
Kh/ks

Mr Paul Gruszniewski
29029 - 112 Avenue, SE

Auburn, WA 98002

USA

Our Reference
(please quote)
T/D — 142 710

Re: Your application regarding your brother, Mr Juda GRUSZNIEWSKI,
born in Lomza (Lomscha) on 13.7.1922

Dear Mr Gruszniewski,

We should like to refer to your letter dated 9th September 1985 and to advise you that on the basis of your particulars, a check was made of our records.

As result of these investigations we herewith enclose an Excerpt from Documents containing all indications available here about the incarceration of your brother.

The following particulars could be taken from the available post-war records:

GRUSZNIEWSKI, Juda, born in Lomza on 13.7.1922,
Nationality: Polish, Religion: Jewish, Marital
status: single, Names of parents: Isak (Iseak)
and Miriam, Last known place of residence: Lomza,
Occupation: technician,
was transferred to the T/B-Sanatorium Amberg on 11th
July 1945 (coming from Concentration Camp Dachau),
died there at 8.45 hours on 18th December 1945,
Cause of death: tuberculosis of the lungs, heart and
circulatory weakness.

./.

(page two of letter)

- 2 -

We regret that we must give you this confirmation of death and ask you to please accept our deepest sympathy.

We shall send you a death certificate later.

Regarding the grave-site, we shall initiate investigations. You will be informed of the result immediately.

We remain

with kind regards,

F. Figge
for the Archives

Enclosure: 1

SERVICE INTERNATIONAL DE RECHERCHES
INTERNATIONAL TRACING SERVICE
INTERNATIONALER SUCHDIENST

D - 3548 AROLSEN

Tel. (05691) 637 — Telegr.-Adr. ITS Arolsen

Notre Réf. Our Ref. T/D – 142 710 Unser Az.	Votre Réf. Your Ref. – – – Ihr Az.	Arolsen, 21st February 1986

EXTRAIT DE DOCUMENTS	EXCERPT FROM DOCUMENTS	DOKUMENTEN-AUSZUG
Il est certifié par la présente que les indications suivantes sont conformes à celles des documents originaux en possession du Service International de Recherches et ne peuvent en aucun cas être modifiées par celui-ci.	It is hereby certified that the following indications are cited exactly as they are found in the documents in the possession of the International Tracing Service. It is not permitted for the international Tracing Service to change original entries.	Es wird hiermit bestätigt, daß die folgenden Angaben den Unterlagen des Internationalen Suchdienstes originalgetreu entnommen sind. Der Internationale Suchdienst ist nicht berechtigt, Originaleintragungen zu ändern.

Nom / Name / Name **GRUSZNIEWSKI -/-**

Prenoms / First names / Vornamen **Juda -/-**

Nationalité / Nationality / Staatsangehörigkeit **Polish -/-**

Date de naissance / Date of birth / Geburtsdatum **13.7.1922 -/-**

Lieu de naissance / Place of birth / Geburtsort **Lomscha -/-**

Religion / Religion / Religion **Jewish -/-**

Noms des parents / Parents' names / Namen der Eltern **Izak and Mirjam nee BRAUSMAN -/-**

Profession / Profession / Beruf **joiner -/-**

Dernière adresse connue / Last known residence / Zuletzt bekannter Wohnsitz **Lomscha, Dluga 8 -/-**

Etat civil / Marital status / Familienstand **single -/-**

Arrêté le / Arrested on / Verhaftet am **5th August 1942 -/-** à / in / in **Blizyn -/-** par / by / durch **not indicated -/-**

Emprisonné / Confined / Eingeliefert **in Concentration Camp Dachau/Commando Kaufering -/-**

No de détenu / Prisoner's No / Häftlingsnummer **119520 -/-**

Le / On / Am **27th October 1944 -/-** venant de / coming from / von **Concentration Camp Auschwitz -/-** par / by / durch **not indicated -/-**

Catégorie / Category / Kategorie **"Sch. (* Schutzhaft), Jude" -/-**

Transféré / Transferred / Überstellt **not indicated; liberated by the American Army as prisoner of Concentration Camp Dachau. -/-**

Indications complémentaires / Further indications / Weitere Angaben **none -/-**

Remarques du SIR / Remarks of the ITS / Bemerkungen des ITS **none -/-**

(page two of letter)

<table>
<tr><td rowspan="6">C</td><td>Staat: BUNDESREPUBLIK DEUTSCHLAND</td><td colspan="2">Gemeinde: Stadt Amberg</td></tr>
<tr><td>Etat: REPUBLIQUE FÉDÉRALE D'ALLEMAGNE</td><td>Staat: BONDSREPUBLIEK DUITSLAND</td><td>(Standesamt Amberg Nr. 1380/1945)</td></tr>
<tr><td>State: FEDERAL REPUBLIC OF GERMANY</td><td>Devlet: FEDERAL ALMANYA CUMHURIYETI</td><td></td></tr>
<tr><td>Estado: REPUBLICA FEDERAL DE ALEMANIA</td><td>Država: SAVEZNA REPUBLIKA NJEMAČKA</td><td></td></tr>
<tr><td>Stato: REPUBBLICA FEDERALE DI GERMANIA</td><td></td><td>Commune de – Municipality – Municipio de – Comune di – Gemeente – Köy veya mahâlle – Opčina</td></tr>
</table>

Auszug aus dem Todesregister

Extrait des registres de l'état civil concernant un décès – Extract of the register of deaths – Extracto del registro de defunciones – Estratto del registro delle morti – Uittreksel uit de registers van de burgerlijke stand omtrent een overlijden – Ölüm kayıt hülâsası sureti – Izvod iz matične knjige umrlih

a)	**Todesort:** lieu de décès – place of death – lugar de fallecimiento – luogo della morte – plaats van overlijden – ölüm yeri – mjesto smrti	A m b e r g
b)	**Todesdatum:** date de décès – date of death – fecha de fallecimiento – data della morte – datum van overlijden – ölüm tarihi – datum smrti	18.12.1945
c)	**Familienname des (der) Verstorbenen:** nom de famille du défunt – surname of the deceased – apellido del difunto – cognome del defunto – familienaam van de overledene – ölünün soyadı – prezime pokojnika	G r u s z n i e w s k i
d)	**Vornamen des (der) Verstorbenen:** prénoms du défunt – christian names of the deceased – nombres de pila del difunto – prenomi del defunto – voornaam(en) van de overledene – ölünün adı – imena pokojnika	Juda
e)	**Geschlecht des (der) Verstorbenen:** sexe du défunt – sex of the deceased – sexo del difunto – sesso del defunto – geslacht van de overledene – ölünün cinsiyeti – spol pokojnika	M
f)	**Geburtsdatum oder Lebensalter des (der) Verstorbenen:** date de naissance du défunt ou âge – date of birth or age of the deceased – fecha del nacimiento o edad del difunto – data della nascita o età del defunto – geboortedatum of leeftijd van de overledene – ölünün doğum tarihi veya yaşı – datum rođenja ili godine starosti pokojnika	13.07.1922
g)	**Geburtsort des (der) Verstorbenen:** lieu de naissance du défunt – place of birth of the deceased – lugar de nacimiento del difunto – luogo della nascita del defunto – geboorteplaats van de overledene – ölünün doğum yeri – mjesto rođenja pokojnika	Lomža
h)	**Letzter Wohnsitz des (der) Verstorbenen:** dernier domicile du défunt – last residence of the deceased – último domicilio del difunto – ultimo domicilio del defunto – laatste woonplaats van de overledene – ölünün son ikametgâhı – posljednje prebivalište pokojnika	A m b e r g
i)	**Name und Vornamen des letzten Ehegatten:** nom et prénoms du dernier conjoint – name and christian names of last spouse – apellido y nombres de pila del último cónyuge – cognome e nome dell'ultimo coniuge – naam en voornamen van de laatste echtgenoot – son eşinin soyadı ve adı – prezime i imena posljednjeg bračnog druga	
j)	**Name und Vornamen des Vaters:** nom et prénoms du père – name and christian names of the father – apellido y nombres de pila del padre – cognome e nome del padre – naam en voornamen van de vader – babasının soyadı ve adı – prezime i imena oca	
k)	**Name und Vornamen der Mutter:** nom et prénoms de la mère – name and christian names of the mother – apellido y nombres de pila de la madre – cognome e nome della madre – naam en voornamen van de moeder – anasının soyadı ve adı – prezime i imena majke	

Ausstellungsdatum, Unterschrift und Dienstsiegel des Registerführers
date de délivrance, signature et sceau du dépositaire
date of issue, signature and seal of keeper
fecha de expedición, firma y sello del depositario
data in cui è stato rilasciato l'atto, con firma e bollo dell'ufficio
datum van afgifte, ondertekening en zegel van de bewaarder
verildiği tarih, nüfus (ahvali şahsiye) memurunun imzası ve mührü
datum izdavanja, potpis i pečat matičara

(Siegel)

A m b e r g

08.04.1986

den

Der Standesbeamte

Internationale Sterbeurkunde